AMY ORR-EWING

Is Believing in God Irrational?

Foreword by Ravi Zacharias

IVP Books

An imprint of InterVarsity Press
Downers Grove, Illinois

InterVarsity Press
P.O. Box 1400, Downers Grove, IL 60515-1426
World Wide Web: www.ivpress.com
E-mail: email@ivpress.com

InterVarsity Press® *is the book-publishing division of InterVarsity Christian Fellowship/USA*®*, a student movement active on campus at hundreds of universities, colleges and schools of nursing in the United States of America, and a member movement of the International Fellowship of Evangelical Students. For information about local and regional activities, write Public Relations Dept., InterVarsity Christian Fellowship/USA, 6400 Schroeder Rd., P.O. Box 7895, Madison, WI 53707-7895, or visit the IVCF website at <www.intervarsity.org>.*

All Scripture quotations, unless otherwise indicated, are taken from the Holy Bible, New International Version®. NIV®. *Copyright ©1973, 1978, 1984 by International Bible Society. Used by permission of Zondervan Publishing House. All rights reserved.*

Published in association with the literary agency of Wolgemuth & Associates, Inc. Published in the United Kingdom by Inter-Varsity Press, Nottingham, under the title But Is It Real?

Design: Cindy Kiple

Images: Ray Massey/Getty Images

ISBN 978-0-8308-3353-5

Printed in the United States of America ∞

Library of Congress Cataloging-in-Publication Data

Orr-Ewing, Amy.
  Is believing in God irrational? / Amy Orr-Ewing.
    p. cm.
  Includes bibliographical references.
  ISBN 978-0-8308-3353-5 (pbk. : alk. paper)
  1. Apologetics. 2. God (Christianity) I. Title.
  BT1103.O77 2008
  239—dc22

                                                                    2008022650

P 23 22 21 20 19 18 17 16 15 14 13 12 11 10 9 8 7 6 5 4 3 2 1

Y 27 26 25 24 23 22 21 20 19 18 17 16 15 14 13 12 11 10 09 08

Contents

Foreword

Some years ago I was on a flight from Brisbane to Sydney, Australia. A young lady sitting next to me was very quiet and, in fact, looked somewhat troubled. I tried to make conversation but didn't succeed. She happened to ask me what I was doing in Sydney and I told her I was there on a speaking trip. "On what?" she asked. "Answering life's deepest questions," I said. There was silence, and then she asked a question about death and its immediate aftermath. We got into a fascinating conversation, but soon we were touching down in Sydney. "When will you be coming back to Brisbane?" I asked. It was not to be for another two months as she was visiting her boyfriend in San Francisco for that period. I gave her a telephone number of a missionary in Brisbane that I thought she should contact on her return.

Two or three years went by, and I returned to Brisbane for some meetings. The missionary said to me, "I have a surprise guest for dinner tonight who wants to see you." Wondering who it could be, I was utterly surprised to find out it was this young lady. She was now married to the gentleman from San

Francisco, and they were both in seminary preparing to go as missionaries to India.

"What on earth happened?" I asked. Well, as it went, she got back from the United States and the first Wednesday she was in town she showed up in church, looking for the missionary I had asked her to meet. Her first encounter at church was a shock to her. *These people actually think they are talking to God when they pray,* she thought. But something in her heart kept tugging away that she should keep returning. Two weeks later, the missionary was leaving on furlough and introduced her to the person taking his place. To make a long story short, in a few weeks she committed her life to Christ, then introduced her fiancé to him, and Brisbane was where they were now studying.

"What made you ask me about death on that flight we were on?" I asked her. "I had just buried my father the previous week," she said, "and the question haunted me as to where he was."

Having traveled the globe for over three decades, I have encountered such scenarios time and again, for they are both unique and universal. I can attest that often our most profound and deeply felt questions are born out of such life-defining experiences. And I have very little doubt that the prodigal son ultimately did not come home because of some incredibly designed argument; instead, his memory of home and all that he had lost in a relationship began his homeward trek. His home was where his hungers were met. The "far country" is where his hungers intensified.

My colleague Amy Orr-Ewing takes you on a journey to where the soul is at home with its hungers of mind and heart fulfilled. As our world becomes more uncertain and fearsome, there is a longing not only for verbal answers but for a sense of belonging and what Jesus called "rest for the soul." "Take my yoke upon you and learn from me, for I am gentle and humble in heart, and you will find rest for your souls. For my yoke is easy and my burden is light" (Matthew 11:29-30). I have been thinking so much of those verses of late—maybe even more so because I sense and see so much of the opposite in the times in which we live. We are made to be burden-bearers; we are meant to be under a yoke and find our peace within that legitimate weight we carry. We cannot live out our lives isolated from others; we cannot be free from the bearing of burdens. The longing of the human heart is to know to whom we should be yoked, whose burden we should be carrying, and how to lighten the load of another without making our own unbearable. The eyes we look into and the faces we see in the audiences across the world reflect this longing more and more.

These are the very "soulish" questions that Amy has encountered in conversations in the past couple of years and addresses in this book. Amy is one of the most sought-after speakers in Europe today, and increasingly so in North America, no doubt due in part to her seeking mind and humble heart. She writes, "I discovered during my journey of talking to the many people who have asked me all of the questions in this book that finding answers is a real challenge because the questions do not just touch on intellectual ideas but are nuanced with emotional realities and the pain of life." Indeed, like the young Brisbane woman who had questions about death after losing her father, Amy shares how one life-threatening experience as a teenager brought similar bewildering questions for her to the surface: Is God really with me, and does he have a purpose for my life?

Whether in her recent BBC debate on the resurrection or with a university student struggling to comprehend God's love, Amy speaks with clarity and compassion. The questions she has addressed reveal the very title of this book: whether the Christian faith is all merely ideational and out of touch with the sharp edges of reality. Anyone who has asked honest questions in such matters will relate to these issues. What I would like the reader to know is that the answers come from one who not merely listens but also feels and embodies the answers.

I recall on one campus some years ago finishing a tough series of meetings. On the day I was departing from that city, my host mentioned to me that he had brought his neighbor, a medical doctor, to the last meeting. "She is a skeptic through and through," he said. "Would you like to know what her response was to your presentation last night?" he asked. Knowing full well that I had no choice, I answered rather eagerly in the affirmative. This was his reply of her sentiments: "Powerful . . . simply powerful. . . . I wonder what he's like in his private life." That was her one-line response to a three-hour evening. In short, the entire weight of the argument rested, for her, on the coherence between the argument and the enfleshing of that argument. The reasoning was not good enough. The practical impact in the private life of the reasoner was the final test.

For those of us who know Amy and have watched her life, we see there is no breakdown of that sort. She lives her message and is a powerful example of the truths she presents. She meets the test of reality, and that is what makes this book so arguably real.

Ravi Zacharias
Author and speaker

Introduction

It was strange walking down a hospital corridor with a growing sense of foreboding, getting closer to the consultant's office and wondering what he would say. I was fifteen years old and had the afternoon off school to receive the results from the operation I had undergone the week before. A mole on my leg had begun to turn dark, and my doctor had decided to remove it as a precaution. My mother and I entered the office together and sat down. The consultant leaned over the desk and said, "I'm afraid it's cancer."

Those words still echo in my head now as I write them; the shock, the fear, the bewildering emotions rushed through my body from head to toe. He went on to explain that it was, in fact, a borderline case of melanoma and that they would need to do a further operation to make absolutely sure that I was in the clear. But those stark words "it's cancer" stayed with me. What was life all about? What was it for? Was there a purpose for my life? Was my life over?

Well, as you have probably guessed, I survived. My life was not yet over; it was to last more than fifteen years. Through the experience of the cancer, I encountered a God who is near us in suffering, a God who makes his presence known. I remember lying in my bed, shaking with fear and calling out to God, who then tangibly filled my bedroom and lifted the fear and blackness from my chest. As Psalm 30:1-3 says,

I will exalt you, O LORD,
> for you lifted me out of the depths
> and did not let my enemies gloat over me.
O LORD my God, I called to you for help
> and you healed me.
O LORD, you brought me up from the grave;
> you spared me from going down into the pit.

As life has gone on, friends have died suddenly, members of my community in London have been on the receiving end of horrific violence, and the questions of the human heart have kept on coming year after year as I have traveled and met people of different ages, backgrounds and nationalities.

I have found that many people have questions about Christian experience. These questions can be genuine objections to Christianity or things that trouble Christians in the back of their minds. During my journey of talking to the many people who have asked me all the questions in this book, I've discovered that finding answers is a real challenge because the questions do not just touch on intellectual ideas but are undergirded by emotional realities and the pain of life. The issues examined in this book have all emerged during conversations in the course of the last couple of years.

Is God real? Is it possible to know anything—let alone to know him? Why do bad things happen to people who worship this God? What about the spiritual experiences of other faiths? All these questions and more have come out of real-life situations, so whether you are an atheist or someone who wonders if there just might be something more to Christianity than you first thought, I hope that, as you read this book, at least some of the thoughts offered here will help you to see what the Christian faith has to say amid all the pain, confusion and complexity of life.

1

What About Other People's Genuine Experience of God?

A few years ago, an Oxford student asked if I would come and talk with his friend Jack, who had some questions about Christianity. We arranged a time to meet, and on a gray October Monday afternoon we sheltered from the rain in a coffee shop. At first it was a little awkward—we all knew why we were there, but being English, we skirted around the subject of God and chatted about the weather, the improving quality of hot drinks in Oxford's cafés and a number of other trivial subjects.

After a little while, Jack began tentatively to ask questions about Christianity. We talked about the nature of proof, whether science had dispensed with God, and the problem of suffering. It seemed quite difficult to make any progress because as soon as I answered one question another unrelated issue would be brought up. As I was beginning to wonder whether this was purely an intellectual exercise or really a genuine search for answers, I said, "I've tried to answer all your questions, and I've asked quite a few myself, so tell me, what do you feel your most important question is?"

The guy didn't miss a beat. "My Christian friends claim to have a relationship with God and assert that Jesus is the only way to come to God. Isn't it arrogant, even ridiculous, to nullify the genuine experience of Tibetan monks on the basis of your own experience. How can you say that your experience of God is real and theirs isn't?"

One of the reasons this question is so powerful is that, at its heart, Christianity really *is* all about a personal relationship with a living God and these ideas are in direct contra-distinction to the fundamental beliefs of Buddhist monks. If Christianity is primarily about relationship with God through Jesus Christ, what is Buddhism all about? A brief synopsis may be helpful here for those less familiar with Buddhist ideas.

BUDDHISM

The Buddha, which means enlightened one, was born as Siddhartha Gautama in Lumbini (in present–day Nepal) into a wealthy princely family of the Sakya clan. The date of his birth is variously placed between 624 and 448 B.C., but the commonly accepted date is 560 B.C. Guatama renounced his comfortable life at the age of twenty-nine and lived the life of a traveling sage, seeking out teachers who could instruct him. At the age of thirty-six, during the full moon night of May, he received what he believed was enlightenment. This happened in Gaya (in present-day India). During the full moon night of July he delivered his first discourse near Varanasi, introducing the world to the "Four Noble Truths." At age eighty, he died, and his death is referred to as *Parinibbana*, or final release.

The Buddha's teaching is encapsulated in his Four Noble Truths:

1. The noble truth of *dukkha* (suffering, stress): this word is notoriously difficult to render accurately in English, but it seems to encapsulate the idea that life is fundamentally fraught with suffering and disappointment of every possible description.

2. The noble truth of the cause of *dukkha:* the cause of this suffering and dissatisfaction is *tanha* (desire) in all its forms.

3. The noble truth of the cessation of *dukkha:* an end to all suffering and dissatisfaction can be found through the abandonment of desire.

4. The noble truth of the path leading to the cessation of *dukkha*: there is a method of achieving the end of all suffering, which is called the "Noble Eightfold Path."

To each of these "noble truths" the Buddha assigned a specific task that the follower is to carry out: the first noble truth is to be comprehended; the second is to be abandoned; the third is to be realized; the fourth is to be developed. The full realization of the third noble truth paves the way for nirvana, the transcendent freedom that stands as the final goal of all the Buddha's teachings.

The Noble Eightfold Path is intended to deliver us from unhappiness and to help us find release, once and for all, from the painful and exhausting cycle of birth and death *(samsara)*. Buddhism teaches that because of our ignorance (*avijja*) of the Four Noble Truths we have been bound for countless eons in this cycle. The Noble Eightfold Path offers a comprehensive practical guide to the development of the qualities and skills in the human heart that need to be cultivated in order to bring the practitioner to the final goal, the supreme freedom and happiness of nirvana. This means total oneness with Brahman—the impersonal Ultimate Reality.

If Buddhism is about the ultimate extinguishing of the individual into the One, Christianity is about a personal God who invites people into relationship with himself. These two rival claims could not be more divergent on this crucial idea of "experience" or the related idea of "relationship." To the Buddhist, human experience is part of the *dukkha* (suffering), which is dealt with by extinguishing all desire.

Now, this is a difficult idea to grasp, since it is appears to be essentially self-contradictory: to want to get rid of desire is itself a desire. However, at its heart Buddhism is a religion guiding its followers through a process, the end aim of which is to lose one's sense of experience, emotion, and even personhood, and self to attain oneness with the impersonal One. So, as we come back to the original question, we can see that any talk about Tibetan monks' "experience of God" is to misconstrue Buddhism entirely.

CHRISTIANITY

In contrast, the heart of Christianity is God making an appeal of love to the human beings he has created. Through his son Jesus' sacrificial death on the cross, all the sin and rubbish that would stand between an ordinary human and a holy God can be forgiven and dealt with. But the offer is more than forgiveness—it is reconciliation. Christians are called "children of God" (see Romans 8:16) because the forgiveness received opens the way for relationship with this loving God. This relationship is real and is genuinely experienced in the life of the believer. I can no more deny the reality of my relationship with God than I can my relationship with my best friend who lives around the corner. Although I cannot see God, I can know him. This is the testimony of Christians throughout the ages.

There are so many examples of different kinds of people we could draw on to illustrate this. One of these is a man named Chuck Colson. He was an ex-Marine captain and President Nixon's White House hatchet man, and he ended up going to prison for his part in the Watergate scandal. In the midst of his gripping life story, he talks of his search for God: "I guess I'm looking for something. . . . I'm trying to find out what's real and what isn't—who we are—who I am in relation to God." When he finally committed his life to Christ in December 1973, there were shock waves in Washington as many suspected a gimmick, but this unlikely convert had truly encountered God through Jesus Christ.

> And so early that Friday morning, while I sat alone staring at the sea I love, words I had not been certain I could understand or say fell naturally from my lips: "Lord Jesus Christ, I believe You. I accept You. Please come into my life. I commit it to You." With these few words that morning, while the briny sea churned, came a sureness of mind that matched the depth of feeling in my heart. There came something more: strength and serenity, a

wonderful new assurance about life, a fresh perception of myself and the world around me. . . . I was coming alive to things I'd never seen before; as if God was filling the barren void I'd known for so many months.[1]

Colson's life was completely transformed by this, and although he did go to prison for what he had done, he went on to found Prison Fellowship, which works with prisoners around the world, reaching out to those in need. A real encounter with God through Christ is the beginning of a relationship that the believer experiences in a real way. This is what Christianity lived out day-to-day is all about.

We can see that Buddhism and Christianity have very different approaches to—and indeed frames of reference for—the very concept of experience, and so it is not surprising that one would seem to negate the other. It is better to be open and honest about this difference than to try to relativize or homogenize all the religions of the world so that they can appear to be the same.

But if the friend I had met in the café had asked about Muslim experience rather than Tibetan monks, wouldn't the answer have been different? Well, of course Islam is very different from Buddhism, but it is also fundamentally different from Christianity.

ISLAM

The doctrine of God within Islam is most significantly encapsulated in the important term *tauhid*. This word refers to faith in the principle that is at the very heart of Islam: the concept of Allah as one. God is unity itself. A universal Islamic declaration was made at the opening of the International Islamic Conference on April 12, 1980, affirming that

> oneness of Allah *(Tauhid)* is the foundation of Islam. It affirms that Allah and Allah alone is our Creator, Sustainer, Guide and Lord: that He has no partners: that His will is supreme and encompasses the entire universe; that He is the Law Giver and to Him we must submit and surrender.[2]

Islam's perception of God, as put forward in the Qur'an, is that he is majestic and utterly transcendent. He is awesome and powerful, commanding all that he has made. He is not portrayed as a relational being in his essence, as the trinitarian God of the Bible is.

Within Christianity the statement "God is love" applies to the being of God in distinction from his creation. Before God creates, he is already love; Father, Son and Holy Spirit love one another within the being of God from all eternity. Humans are then created and welcomed into relationship with God. The Islamic God is One; he is portrayed as loving his creatures, but love is not an essential part of his nature, because before he creates, there is no one to love. The Islamic God is primarily transcendent and secondarily loving once he has created.

The Qur'an is focused on the idea of submission to this transcendent God rather than personal relationship with him.[3] This is not a pejorative statement about Islam, since for Muslims God's strength and beauty, his "otherness," are key. For the Muslim, the perceived weakness of Christianity is the anthropomorphizing of God. This is especially relevant to the idea of God's love costing him as much as it does in Christianity; this idea of God's love seems to bring shame on God, and for a Muslim that is a travesty. One Muslim author observes,

> Beyond their speculations concerning God, the necessity of his existence, and his properties, Muslim theologians and philosophers have apparently felt no need to question the possibility and reality of a human experience of God. . . . It is even difficult to find an appropriate Arabic or Persian expression for "experience of God" without running the risk of encroaching on the absolute transcendence of the God of Islam, of anthropomorphizing him.[4]

The God of Islam should not be talked about in personal or humanized terms; to do so is to undermine the nature of Muhammad's perception of the nature of God and to risk misunderstanding the Qur'an entirely.

Neither Buddhism nor Islam have an equivalent to the idea of relationship with God, which is at the heart of the Christian message—it is, in fact, unique. This is why Christian testimony—a personal account of one's relationship with God—underlines the uniqueness of Jesus rather than begging the question, What about other people's experiences; aren't they genuine too?

The differences affirmed here between the approaches of Islam, Buddhism and Christianity on the issue of experience help us to navigate the genuine distinctions and opposing truth claims that do really exist. But underlying my friend's question at the beginning of this chapter was the basic assumption that these differences are not important—as if all the religions are a melting pot of skewed "faith-based" views that can be lumped together.

The exception to this paradigm is a secular worldview that is uncritically accepted as being entirely unbiased and neutral in its approach. The Indian Christian apologist Ravi Zacharias helpfully comments that, in our postmodern society, many people like to believe that all the religions are fundamentally the same but just superficially different, whereas in reality they are just superficially similar but fundamentally different. As one poet put it,

We believe there's something in horoscopes,
UFO's and bent spoons;
Jesus was a good man just like Buddha,
Mohammed and ourselves.
We believe he was a good moral teacher but we think
His good morals are really bad.

We believe that all religions are basically the same,
at least the one we read was.
They all believe in love and goodness.
They only differ on matters of creation,
sin, heaven, hell, God and salvation.[5]

This helpful observation is true of this whole area of experience of God. However, many people in our society believe that to claim that Jesus is uniquely the way to God is somehow shockingly intolerant. If Christian experience is startlingly different and unique when laid alongside comparable alternatives, isn't it still intolerant and even arrogant to assert that this somehow nullifies the others?

TOLERANCE

Tolerance of other people's views is a highly prized virtue in our culture, and when talking about religion it has come to mean accepting that all religions are equally true or untrue. No distinctions can be made. But what does tolerance actually mean? A helpful definition of *tolerate* is to "allow (something one dislikes or disagrees with) to exist without interference . . . [or to] patiently endure (something unpleasant)."[6]

The important fact here is that tolerance is needed for people who have different opinions. If I agree that your path leads to God as much as mine, I don't need to be tolerant because we agree. It is only if I disagree that I need to be tolerant toward another person's view. Yet Christianity is perceived as being intolerant. After all, isn't it wrong to say that somebody else is wrong? Of course the ironic thing is that the person saying that it is wrong to say that someone else is wrong is also saying that Christians are wrong for saying what they believe! Therefore, the crucial question at issue here is not whether Christian belief is tolerant or not but whether it is true and real.

ARROGANCE

Another objection to Christian uniqueness is that it is arrogant to say that Jesus is the only way to God. This point is often made using the Indian story of an elephant in the jungle. Different blind scribes come up to the elephant and take hold of the different body parts. One holds the trunk and declares, "This is a snake." Another holds the leg and says, "You are wrong. It is not a snake, it is a tree trunk!" Still another holds the tail and says, "You are both wrong. It is a rope." The different individuals represent the religions of the world, and the moral of the story is that no one faith has the whole truth; it would be arrogant to claim it. All have a little piece.

The intriguing thing about this parable is that there are two important differences between the person telling the story and the people inside the story. The first is a difference in perspective: the people inside the story are close up to the elephant, but the storyteller is standing back and has the whole picture.

The second difference is more fundamental: the people inside the story are blind, and the person telling the story can see. The clear implication of this story is that Jesus, Buddha, Krishna, Muhammad and Moses were blind, but the storyteller can see. Who sounds arrogant now? Is it not just as arrogant to claim that you know that all paths lead to God as it is to claim that you agree with Jesus that he is the only way to God?

Thus the real debate is not about who is arrogant or not, but instead explores what is actually true and real. The issue on which you reject Christianity should not be arrogance, since surely it is just as arrogant to say that all paths lead to God as it is to say that none lead there. The question is not whether it is arrogant to say that Jesus is the way to God—but is it actually true? Is it real?

EXCLUSION

Another motivation or moral force behind questioning the unique truth claim that Jesus makes is that of exclusion. "How can you, the Christian, exclude all these religions?" Again we need to think carefully about this, because the reality is that whatever position we hold, we exclude some views. Even the person who believes that all ways lead to God—which to be consistent, therefore, must include the ideologies of people such as Idi Amin, Pol Pot, Stalin and Osama bin Laden—by that very position excludes the view that only some ways lead to God or only one way leads to God.

In the same way, the average tolerant person with whom we are all friends would probably want to exclude the extreme views of Hitler or Milosević and therefore would believe that only *some* ways lead to God—perhaps the five main world religions. This position excludes the view that *all* ways lead to God or that *one* way leads to God. And the Christian who wants to say, "I follow Jesus and he said that he is the only way to the Father," excludes the view that *all* ways or *some* ways lead to God. Every view excludes some, so the key issue at stake is not who is excluding people, but what is actually true and real.

No matter how hard you try, you can't escape the fact that one truth claim will always exclude some possibilities.

- The person who says that all ways to God are true excludes the possibility that only one way or only some ways are true.

- The person who says that some ways to God are true excludes the possibility that only one way or all ways to God are true.

- The person who says that only one way to God is true then also excludes others.

All views exclude, and so it seems a little unreasonable to single out Christianity and reject it on the basis that it excludes.

Sometimes the objection to Christianity as "the truth" may be phrased as a common generalization "All truth is relative"—

except that statement itself, of course. Roger Scruton, research professor for the Institute for the Psychological Sciences, famously put it this way, "A writer who says there are no truths . . . is asking you not to believe him. So don't."[7]

And so we come back to the original question: What about other people's experiences; are they somehow invalidated by me believing in Jesus as the only way to God? As we have seen, other religious paths do not make claims about personal experience of a personal God, and so it is difficult to compare experience with nonexperience. We do, however, come to the issue of sincerity. I believe that it is possible to treat a person with a different viewpoint with tolerance and respect, not questioning the sincerity of his or her belief but nonetheless disagreeing with the content of that belief. Having considered some of the differences between competing worldview claims on the question of experience at a theoretical level, we are left with another more pragmatic approach to consider.

At the end of the day, any claims of encounter with God and real relationship with Jesus Christ are open to testable firsthand experience for every living person. Christians believe that a simple step of opening one's heart and mind to God is all that it takes to begin a lifelong relationship with him. The Bible promises that if we draw near to God, he will draw near to us. This is a clear invitation to encounter God. A simple prayer like "God, if you are there, please reveal yourself to me" can be an intriguing beginning of our search for him.

However, if this question of whether the Christian claim to experience God undermines other alternatives can be answered, shouldn't that experience of God itself be questioned? Couldn't the whole idea of God be a delusion?

2

Your "Experience of God"
Is Delusional, Not Real . . .

A number of years ago, my church in Oxford had a baptism service in which one of the men about to go under the water gave a short speech telling everybody why he was about to get into a huge tank of water fully clothed in front of seven hundred people. He began by explaining that his wife had come home a year earlier and announced that she had decided to become a Christian. He was horrified to hear this news and immediately began quizzing her about her new beliefs. Had she been brainwashed? What on earth attracted her to the church in this day and age? What did "a personal relationship with God" mean? Could she feel it? What was the factual basis for Christianity? And on it went.

When his wife told him that she was going to pray regularly, this man had an idea. He decided that he would find out what she was praying about and that over the course of a year he would write down everything she prayed for, with the date of the prayer next to it. On the opposite page he would write down answers to the prayers. Then, at the end of the year, he would hand her the book and show her a book of blank pages, proving that none of her prayers had been answered and that her newfound faith was a delusion. As he told the story, the Christian congregation bristled slightly; the tension in the air was palpable.

The man continued by explaining that at the end of the year, he had a book filled with prayers on one side and answers on the other. The only unanswered prayer from the year was his own conversion to Christianity. Completely blown away by this, he decided to investigate the claims of Christianity for himself, and he found himself convinced both intellectually and now existentially that it was true.

In a "postmodern" society, spirituality is generally seen as a positive thing. People may not be signing up for organized religion in huge numbers, but many do believe in a valuable spiritual dimension to life. In our tolerant age, where every belief is seen as equally valid, the Christian claim to have a personal relationship with God is viewed by many as a lifestyle option that is to be commended if it makes the individual happy. This pluralist approach involves its own challenges. How can Christians share their own personal experience of God with someone else without creating the suspicion that they are trying to "impose their views" on another?

Part of the problem here is that our society seems to have created two categories: spiritual matters, and everything else. Sharing spiritual matters, particularly the claims of Christ and his gospel, is considered intolerant. But it would be considered self-ish and unfriendly to keep to oneself something wonderful and life enhancing within the second category of "everything else."

As a mother of baby twin boys, I experience this in my domestic life. If a local shop begins to stock a limited number of a fantastic toy at an incredibly low price, mothers everywhere call friends to let them know where this great bargain can be found. We don't keep good news about mundane things to ourselves. Why should it be any different when it comes to spiritual matters? If meeting Jesus Christ has transformed my life, why would it be wrong to share that information with others so that they too can find forgiveness and eternal life? If it's true for me, why isn't it also going to be true for them?

GOD—A DELUSION?

However, before we get too far ahead of ourselves, let's consider some prominent voices that reject the validity of the believer's experience of God, claiming that it is a delusion. A delusion is something that people believe in despite a total lack of evidence. Professor Richard Dawkins, who holds the Charles Simonyi Chair for the Public Understanding of Science at Oxford University, writes, "You say you have experienced God directly? Well, some people have experienced a pink elephant but that probably doesn't impress you."[1] For atheists like Dawkins, "religion is scarcely distinguishable from childhood delusions like the 'imaginary friend' and the bogeyman under the bed. Unfortunately, the God delusion possesses adults, and not just a minority of unfortunates in an asylum."[2]

Atheist Sam Harris goes further: "We have names for people who have many beliefs for which there is no rational justification. When their beliefs are extremely common we call them 'religious' otherwise, they are likely to be called 'mad,' 'psychotic,' or 'delusional.' "[3]

On the face of it, this seems like an extraordinary insult in our tolerant age, yet it is important that we not just ignore these wild assertions, but that we listen to and investigate such stark objections to the truthfulness of Christianity. How have the so-called New Atheists, and Dawkins in particular, come to the conclusions they are so widely propagating? Dawkins, Hitchens, Harris, et al., base their assertions that religious believers are deluded on three important ideas about religious faith. They assert

- that evolutionary science has dispensed with God.

- that religious delusion is based on assertion rather than evidence and so cannot be reasoned with and ultimately leads to violence.

- that faith in God is a virus that infects the brain.

SCIENCE DISPENSING WITH GOD

Taking these points, we can begin with the idea that evolutionary science has dispensed with God. Writing in the *Observer* newspaper, the former Bishop of Oxford Richard Harries comments with incredulity on the naive statements often made by atheists, exposing

> their simplistic notion that a scientific approach to life somehow rules out a religious approach. This is plainly false, as the percentage of trained scientists who believe in God is about the same as for the population as a whole.

During my time as Bishop of Oxford, there have always been a number of people with science PhDs offering themselves for ordination.[4]

Dawkins in particular strays into this assumption, failing to apply the same standards of research and evidence to his comments on God that he would expect from anyone commenting on his field of biology.

Dawkins writes with erudition and sophistication on issues of evolutionary biology, clearly having mastered the intricacies of his field and its vast research literature. Yet when he comes to deal with anything to do with God, we seem to enter into a different world. It is the world of a schoolboy debating society, relying on rather heated, enthusiastic, overstatements, spiced up with some striking oversimplifications and more than an occasional misinterpretation (accidental I can only assume) to make some superficially plausible points—the sort of arguments that once persuaded me when I was a schoolboy. But that was then.[5]

The idea that evolutionary science has disposed of God seems to be a strangely shaky basis on which to build one's opposition to theism, since it is so easy to demonstrate—by reading the research of the many scientists who persist in believing in God, Nobel prizes and all—that the science itself does not necessarily exclude God. As one reviewer of Dawkins's work puts it:

This persistence (in belief in God) is what any scientific attack on religion must explain—and this one doesn't. Dawkins mentions lots of modern atheist scientists who have tried to explain the puzzle: Robert Hinde, Scott Atran, Pascal Boyer, D. S. Wilson, Daniel Dennett, all of them worth reading. But he cannot accept the obvious conclusion to draw from their works, which is that thoroughgoing atheism is unnatural and will never be popular.[6]

The fact that so many noted scientists believe in God seems to be a rather basic point to make here, but it does show that overly simplistic assertions that science has completely dispensed with God should be taken with a hefty pinch of salt, if not entirely rejected as empty polemic. As Dr. John Lennox, a reader in mathematics at Oxford University and a fellow in mathematics and philosophy at Green College Oxford, points out,

> We ought . . . to balance the account by citing some eminent scientists who do believe in God. Sir John Houghton FRS writes: "Our science is God's science. He holds the responsibility for the whole scientific story. . . . The remarkable order, consistency, reliability and fascinating complexity found in the scientific description of the universe are reflections of the order, consistency, reliability and complexity of God's activity." Former Director of Kew Gardens Sir Ghilean Prance FRS gives equally clear expression to his faith. "For many years I have believed that God is the great designer behind all nature. . . . All my studies in science since then have confirmed my faith.[7]

But why do Harris, Dawkins and other atheists believe that scientific research has dispensed with any possibility of God existing? What is the basis of their argument, beyond the bare assertion that it is true? Dawkins believes that his atheism is grounded in biology. He argues that since his belief in Darwinian evolution provides an explanation for the complexity of the universe, there is no need for and no place for a designer, and thus God does not exist.

There are many problems with this chain of thought, but for our purposes the important question to raise is that of whether the scientific method, using scientific tools, is able to competently comment on a philosophical question. Atheist Stephen Jay Gould concedes this point: "Science simply cannot (by its legitimate methods) adjudicate the issue of God's possible superintendence of nature."[8]

Dawkins understands this difficulty and in his writing draws on Bertrand Russell's famous analogy that disproving God is as difficult as disproving the speculation that there could be a teapot in space orbiting the moon. It is impossible to say for sure that there isn't one, but we basically know it isn't there, and we don't spend valuable energy looking for it. But this is surely a flimsy basis on which to build such an aggressive edifice of polemic as Dawkins's certainty to deny God's existence.

But Dawkins continues on in his convinced trajectory over the nonexistence of God and takes issue with Gould for implying that scientists cannot comment on the metaphysical, asking, "Why shouldn't we comment on God as scientists?"[9] Surely the logical and correct conclusion in this case is Alister McGrath's: "If the scientific method can neither prove nor disprove the existence or nature of God, then either we abandon the question as unanswerable (something which Dawkins certainly does not choose to do) or we answer it on other grounds."[10]

But this is exactly where Dawkins's arguments begin to fall down. As soon as he ventures outside his area of expertise—human biology—he falls back on tired atheistic arguments and assertions, offering no new ideas or fresh evidence, parodying religion but failing to engage with the philosophical strengths of theism. As Francis Collins, director of the Human Genome Project, puts it, "It becomes readily apparent that Dawkins has aimed his attack at a naive version of faith that most serious believers would not recognize. . . . Dawkins' choice of atheism emerges as the most irrational of the available choices about God's existence."[11]

Furthermore, the New Atheists equate religious belief with irrationality. As John Lennox points out, they strongly believe that " 'supernatural' implies 'non-rational.' " But, he goes on, "to those of us who have engaged in serious theological reflection, this will seem quite wrong-headed: the notion that there is a Creator God is a rational notion, not a non-rational one. To equate 'rational explanation' with 'natural explanation' is at best an indicator of a strong prejudice, at worst a category mistake."[12]

RELIGION AND EVIDENCE

The second plank of the idea that God is a delusion is that religious faith is always based on empty assertion and not evidence. This then raises a number of questions: Is religious faith based purely on assertion rather than evidence? Can it therefore not be reasoned with? Does religion necessarily lead to violence, as Christopher Hitchens assures us it does in his book *God Is Not Great*, devoting a whole chapter to the notion that "religion kills," or as Dawkins tells us in the following?

Disagreements between incompatible beliefs cannot be settled by reasoned argument because reasoned argument is drummed out of those trained in religion from the cradle. Instead, disagreements are settled by other means which, in extreme cases, inevitably become violent. Scientists disagree among themselves but they never fight over their disagreements. They argue about evidence or go out and seek new evidence.[13]

The first important point to make here is that, while many people believe that most conflict is caused by religion, a cursory look at the twentieth century will soon dispel that myth. In the twentieth century, as a result of the rise of Nazi and Communist ideology, more people were killed than in all wars in the previous nineteen centuries put together. How is this any different from people killing in the name of their faith, and if it is not different, doesn't this argument against religion equally demolish atheistic ideologies and atheism itself?

The answer supplied in response to this question is simple: when religious people do evil things, they are acting on the promptings of their faith, but when atheists do so, it has nothing to do with their atheism: "Stalin was an atheist and Hitler probably wasn't, but even if he was . . . the bottom line is very simple. Individual atheists may do evil things but they don't do evil things in the name of atheism."[14] This simply does not stand up, since under Stalin much of the Orthodox priesthood was exterminated solely for being religious leaders, as were the clergy of other religions and literally hundreds of thousands of Baptists. The claim that Stalin's atheism had nothing to do with his actions is unbelievably disingenuous. Dawkins goes on to ask, "Why would anyone go to war for the sake of an absence of belief [atheism]?" One just has to think of the armies of the French Revolution or the Chinese invasion of Tibet to answer that question.

The great irony here is that the Christian worldview is founded on the ideas and teaching of the one who taught "blessed are the peacemakers." From the Christian perspective, it is possible to argue that violence is an abandoning of the very core of the faith and is not a logical outworking of the teaching of the New Testament. Atheism, by contrast, lacks a normative philosophical apparatus for peace. This is not to say that atheists are immoral or unpeaceful or, for that matter, that Christians are moral or peaceful, but rather that the *logical* outworking of the worldview is not always the path followed by individual proponents.

It is also a rather obvious generalization to assert that religious believers are incapable of reasoned argument. How do the New Atheists square this with the sheer fact of thousands of elite philosophers, theologians, political scientists, natural scientists and other academics who brilliantly pursue their disciplines and at the same time believe in God and are able to talk reasonably about him? There have, in fact, been prominent vociferous atheists who have changed their minds in recent times on the issue of God's existence, such as Antony Flew, as stated in his book *There Is a God: How the World's Most Notorious Atheist Changed His Mind* (HarperOne, 2007). Hitchens, Harris, Dawkins and others seem to be falling into exactly the trait they criticize in others: making wild assertions that have no basis in evidence.

The reality is that many Christians and other theists are keen to discuss their ideas and open them up to the scrutiny of others. We may disagree or even find the message wanting, but to assert that Christians are unable to reason is rather like a schoolboy putting his hands over his ears and shouting so as to block out the sound of someone else speaking. *The God Delusion*'s assertion seems itself to be a rather closed-minded, irrational polemic that is unable or unwilling to engage with opponents.

Christianity in its genuine forms has always sought out intelligent unbelievers for debate and interaction. Just look at the apostle Paul; it was his custom to speak about Jesus and debate the claims of Christ in the public squares. This historical example was followed by the early church fathers and apologists and has continued to this day, as Christians throughout the ages have believed that they have a true message that stands up to argument in the public sphere and will not be destroyed by genuine, intelligent and rational debate.

GOD AS A VIRUS OF THE BRAIN

The third plank of New Atheist belief is that faith in God is a virus that infects the brain and should be eliminated. Sam Harris, in his *Letter to a Christian Nation*, concludes,

> As a biological phenomenon, religion is the product of cognitive processes that have deep roots in our evolutionary past. Some researchers have speculated that religion itself may have played an important role in getting large groups of prehistoric humans to socially cohere. If this is true, we can say that religion has served an important purpose. This does not suggest, however, that it serves an important purpose now.[15]

Religion in general is written off here as a construct of the human brain that has served its evolutionary purpose rather than being, as Christianity claims to be, rational, true, relevant and real. However, Dawkins goes one step further than Harris in his rhetoric: "For many people, part of growing up is killing off the virus of faith with a good strong dose of rational thinking. But if an individual doesn't succeed in shaking it off, his mind is stuck in a permanent state of infancy, and there is a real danger that he will infect the next generation."[16]

Or, as Nicholas Humphrey puts it, "We should no more allow parents to teach their children to believe, for example, in the literal truth of the Bible or that planets rule their lives, than we should allow parents to knock their children's teeth out."[17]

But, of course, some would argue, it's not interfering with free speech when atheists pass on their views to their children. Here again we see the double standards of this kind of atheism: I will indoctrinate my children with my assertions, but I object to religious people passing on their beliefs. There is also an unstated belief that the atheist's assumptions are scientifically tested whereas the religious person's are stabs in the dark. We have already seen that this is not the case; science can adequately explain a lot about the world, but some philosophical, metaphysical questions—whether questions about ethics, morality, emotion, thinking, personhood or God—cannot be reduced to biochemical equations. This means that much of the atheist protagonist's own thinking is based on metaphysical assumptions that are just as "unscientific" as a religious person's assumptions. As Lennox concludes,

Inevitably, of course, not only those of us who do science,

but all of us, have to choose the presupposition with which we start. There are not many options—essentially just two. Either human intelligence ultimately owes its origin to mindless matter; or there is a Creator. It is strange that some people claim that it is their intelligence that leads them to prefer the first to the second.[18]

The Oxford University professor of historical theology Alister McGrath presses home the challenge:

> The rhetorically freighted "argument" that God is a virus amounts to little more than thinly veiled insinuation, rather than rigorous evidence-based reasoning. Belief in God is proposed as a malignant infection contaminating otherwise pure minds. Yet the whole idea founders on the rocks of the absence of experimental evidence, the subjectivity of Dawkins' personal value-judgments implicated in assessing what is "good" and "bad" and the circularity of self-referentiality.[19]

We are given no rational reasons to accept that God is a hypothesis rather than atheism; again we are dealing with pure assertion. It may sound technical and imposing, but it is an edifice without foundation. This eerie talk of a "virus" that needs to be killed is powerful rhetoric that would fit comfortably in a totalitarian context, but it does not move us any closer to determining whether belief in God is justified or not—whether God is real or a delusion.

CONCLUSION

As atheists write about the delusion of faith, attacking any basis in rationality or reality, Christianity continues to grow. In fact, the fastest-growing branch of the Christian church is Pentecostalism, a section of the church that emphasizes the individual Christian's direct experience of God. Around the world, there are now over six hundred million adherents, largely in the great urban centers of Asia, Africa and Latin America. In Marxism's traditional stronghold, vibrant, orthodox, experiential Christianity is emerging as the true friend of the poor in these regions. Who are we in the West to pronounce them "deluded"?

This brings us to the heart of the matter. Is it really rational or superior to label another person's experience of God delusional out of hand? I may question the basis of someone's belief and allow her or him to question mine. I may be cautious about the source of someone else's religious experience. I may call into question the link between a rival claim to have experienced God and the doctrines of the adherents' faith. But to deny the validity of someone's experience of God as delusion out of hand without properly engaging with the evidence or rationale for that belief is extraordinary. Furthermore, to do this while failing to examine or admit one's own presuppositions for what they are—metaphysical assumptions—is surely ill advised.[20]

A further related challenge to the idea of God as a delusion is to depict religious faith as a construct of the human mind, arising from the emotional and psychological needs of the believer rather than from anything that actually exists. This approach is an alternative to the outright denial or dismissal of Christian experience that we have been analyzing here and instead attempts to rationalize belief in God as "psychological projection." This is what the next chapter will be examining.

3

Your Relationship with God Is Just a Psychological Crutch!

Has anyone ever told you that your faith is a "crutch"? I remember getting into a black taxi outside a central London church. The cabbie took one look at my Bible and launched into his opinion of Christianity. He explained to me with pity and pathos that belief in God is a crutch for weak, pathetic people who don't have the strength to take responsibility for their own lives.

When he finished his lengthy thesis, he looked at me in the mirror as if expecting my response. When I answered, "Thank you very much," with just a hint of irony, he blustered on, likely hoping to increase the diminishing likelihood of a tip with, "Well, I'm just saying it for your own good. A girl like you doesn't need religion!"

This idea that Christian faith is a psychological crutch for needy people is a pervasive one. At its root are a number of assumptions. The first is that God is merely a psychological projection. He doesn't actually exist, not in any real sense; he exists only in the minds of his followers. In fact, the thinking goes, these minds have created him out of their own need. That could be a need for a father figure or a need to give significance to existence by believing in a God who created the world.

Where does this idea come from—this concept of God as a creation or projection of human minds that is propounded by so many? Its most famous proponent was the thinker Sigmund Freud (1856-1939). Freud was an Austrian neurologist and the founder of psychoanalysis, a movement that popularized the theory that unconscious motives control much human behavior. His theories and his treatment of patients were controversial in nineteenth-century Vienna and remain hotly debated today. His research was wide ranging and complex, but for our purposes we examine in particular his commitment to the notion of God as entirely a projection of the human mind.

GOD AS PSYCHOLOGICAL PROJECTION

Though a Jew, Freud was an atheist for most of his life. He went through a brief period of "wavering" on the issue of God in his university days—during which time he wrote to a friend, "The bad part of it, especially for me, lies in the fact that science of all things seems to demand the existence of a God"[1]—yet he emerged from his studies without religious conviction. Freud's peers, and many authors of the time, were immersed in scientific materialism, and he remained a strident atheist. Another factor may have been the appalling anti-Semitism that swept through his native and culturally Roman Catholic Austria. In the light of his experiences of the weakness of Christianity at repelling such vitriol, one writer comments, "One can understand Freud's motivation to discredit and destroy what he called the 'religious *Weltanschauung* (worldview)' and why he referred to religion as 'the enemy.' "[2]

In arguing against the existence of God, Freud believed that an individual's perspective on what God is like sprung from his or her experience of their own father. When people grow up and find themselves alone in the world they cannot go on looking to human parents for security but must find some other more ultimate source of security and end up positing a God to fill this role.

He argued that it is this human need to rise above the vulnerability and frailty of adult existence that leads to us positing the existence of some higher power or God: "When the growing individual finds that he is destined to remain a child for ever, that he can never do without protection against strange superior powers, he lends those powers the features belonging to the figure of his father."[3]

From this perspective, God is merely a creation of the human mind, a projection emanating from human need and desire rather than a distinct reality or being that exists independently of the human mind. Freud's notion of God acting as an idealized father figure for humans, providing a cushion from the harshness of the real world and a comforting friend in the midst of life's troubles, reduces God to a human construct. Indeed, for Freud, God is made in humanity's own image and is the "ultimate wish-fulfillment"; God does not actually exist but is merely the creation of humanity's imagination and desire for a loving father figure.[4]

How might a Christian respond to this? Can God really be explained away so easily by one aspect of psychology? Of course, the most obvious point to make in response is that this argument about projection cuts both ways. After all, isn't it equally possible to say that Freud and other atheists deny the existence of God out of a need to escape from a father figure, or to argue that the nonexistence of God springs from a deep-seated desire for no father figure to exist?

Clearly this doesn't prove that God is real, but it does help us see that Freud's arguments cannot prove that God does not exist, while at the same time helping us tackle the question of projection. After all, dismissing God as a psychological projection while claiming neutrality in our own psyche is disingenuous at best and cannot be an adequate basis for rejecting God. This is rather like the mother who sees her child swearing and is so overcome with fury that she ends up swearing at her child while telling him off. When her child asks about this inconsistency, she replies, "Don't do what I do, do what I say!" We may well cringe inwardly when we hear something like this in a supermarket or airplane, but trying to do away with God as if he were a psychological projection is actually rather similar. The protagonist is saying that you as a Christian are subject to psychological factors but I, the skeptic, am not.

It also becomes quickly apparent that a Freudian belief in God as a human projection cannot provide us with an explanation for the Christian faith of converts who would rather not believe but find themselves compelled by evidence. I have known many people who have started out as strongly convinced nonbelievers but have found that when they looked at real evidence of God and began to read the Bible, they found themselves convinced—almost against their will—that it is actually true and real. It is then that a decision must be made: will I now respond to what I believe is true, or will I sweep it under the carpet? Alister McGrath writes,

> Back in the 1960s, we were told that religion was fading away, to be replaced by a secular world. For some of us that sounded like a great thing. I was an atheist back in the late 1960s, and remember looking forward to the demise of religion with a certain grim pleasure. I had grown up in Northern Ireland, and had known religious tensions and violence at first hand. . . . The future was bright and godless. . . . I started out as an atheist, who went on to become a Christian. I had originally intended to spend my life in scientific research, but found that my discovery of Christianity led me to study its history and ideas in greater depth. I gained my doctorate in molecular biophysics while working in the Oxford laboratories of Sir George Radda, but then gave up active scientific research to study theology.[5]

In fact, we may go further than nullifying this argument that God is a projection of the mind by turning it on its head and suggesting that a desire for a God who can fulfill our needs and provide moral order exists precisely because human beings have been designed and created to desire them. The man floating on a raft at sea is unbearably thirsty, but he won't just get a drink of water simply by being thirsty. But the very existence of his thirst does show that a way for his desire to be satisfied actually exists: fresh water. As C. S. Lewis put it, "Creatures are not born with desires unless satisfaction for those desires exists."[6]

Lewis is an interesting case here because he was a contemporary of Freud and an atheist himself into his thirties. He famously described his unhappiness before turning to Christ as resulting from "an unsatisfied desire which is itself more desirable than any other satisfaction."[7] Lewis described this desire as "Joy," and he spoke of finding it for himself when he surrendered to God: "To be united with that Life in the eternal Sonship of Christ is . . . the only thing worth a moment's consideration."[8] He argued that the inborn longing one feels as a human being is a desire for a relationship with the Creator God and that the very presence of this desire within us suggests the existence of God.

While Freud believed that human desire could be fulfilled in the ordinary run of life, Lewis argued that "earthly pleasures were never meant to satisfy it but only to arouse it, to suggest the real thing. If that is so, I must take care . . . never to mistake them [earthly pleasures] for the something else of which they are only a kind of copy, or echo, or mirage."[9] For the Christian it is a relationship with God that brings humans this genuine fulfillment. The French mathematician Blaise Pascal put it beautifully:

> There once was in man a true happiness, of which all that now remains is the empty print and trace. This he tries in vain to fill with everything around him, seeking in things that are not there the help he cannot find in those that are, though none can help, because the infinite abyss can be filled only with an infinite and immutable object; in other words, by God himself.[10]

St. Augustine famously said of God, "Thou movest us to delight in praising You; for You have formed us for Yourself, and our hearts are restless till they find rest in You."[11] And Woody Allen mused on this from the opposite perspective when he said as an atheist analyzing life, "More than any other time in history, mankind faces a crossroads. One path leads to despair and utter hopelessness. The other, to total extinction. Let us pray we have the wisdom to choose correctly."[12]

And so we have seen that God cannot be dispensed with as if he were a mere psychological projection without atheism being equally treated as the same. But more than that, the desire for God, rather than undermining his existence, points to its reality. After all, if human beings are created by God in his image as the Bible teaches, shouldn't we expect a divine fingerprint and the possibility of relationship between creature and Creator?

However, ultimately for the Christian the important question is not whether I have a psychological need for a father figure or a desire for a father figure not to exist. Rather, the question is about what actually exists: is God really there? The way to come to any conclusions about that is to investigate the evidence for his existence.[13]

So we have observed that the first assumption in the statement "Your relationship with God is just a psychological crutch!" is that God is merely a psychological projection. The second assumption that we encounter is that, because belief in God provides the faithful with a crutch, it is somehow suspect.

GOD AS TALISMAN

The skeptic implies that since the believer finds protection from the cruelty and evil of the world, the idea of God is like a talisman, an irrational superstition. Freud makes the same point: "religious ideas have arisen from the same need as have all other achievements of civilization: from the necessity of defending oneself against the crushingly superior force of nature."[14] Humans need to find comfort and meaning in the midst of the pain of life as well as a guide for how to live, and they look to God for this. The religious believer views the evolution of morality within human societies as moral absolutes revealed and upheld by God. This belief in absolutes then provides an unreal but comforting refuge in a dark world, so that the individual can feel safe in his or her own status before God and secure in the knowledge that evildoers will be punished.

Freud argues against what he sees as an unreal supernatural power who arbitrarily imposes moral standards on humans. For him, God exists only inside the human mind and has been imagined into existence at the whim of carnal desires. He writes, "We shall tell ourselves that it would be very nice if there were a God who created the world and was a benevolent Providence, and if there were a moral order in the universe and an after-life; but it is the very striking fact that all this is exactly as we are bound to wish it to be."[15] Later he states,

> Since it is an awkward task to separate what God himself has demanded from what can be traced to the authority of an all-powerful parliament or a high judiciary, it would be an undoubted advantage if we were to leave God out altogether and honestly admit the purely human origin of all the regulations and precepts of civilization.[16]

One writer comments: "Humans, now educated and enlightened by science, begin to grow out of their childlike belief in God and recognize morals as man-made rules put into place for their own benefit. . . . Freud believed that as education increased and scientific research continued, humans would slowly stop believing in God and begin to recognize that God was simply an expression of their wishes."[17] But if belief in God makes sense of the world and provides a positive moral framework that helps people to live constructively, that in itself is not a reason to disbelieve in him. Similarly, if relationship with God enables the believer to find healing, wholeness and comfort in the midst of their human suffering, we should not be surprised. After all, clearly, if God is real it will have a massive impact on life and on the experience of life.

ONLY FOR THE WEAK AND INFERIOR

The third assumption is that people who make use of this "crutch" of relationship with God, and find it practical, meaningful and effective, must be weak or inferior. This is a rather strange idea, since surely it makes sense to access real sources of support and relationship that are there for us. This reminds me of the story of a man who had been given a suitcase filled with money. He was told that if he could successfully give away this money, he would receive the same amount again for himself. The only condition was that each banknote had to go to a different person. So he thought to himself, *This will be easy. I'm going to be rich!* He ran out into the nearest shopping street, opened his suitcase and started shouting, "Roll up, roll up— free money—absolutely no catch. Come and take it."

Most people passed straight by, not even looking at him. A few slowed their pace but thought better of it. One woman stopped and asked, "What's the catch? What are you going to try to get out of me?"

"Absolutely nothing," the man replied. "It really is free money. Please take it."

"No, I don't think so," she said, and walked off. A very small proportion of the shoppers on that day took the free money. They were so suspicious as to be convinced that no deal could really be that simple and easy. The money really was free, with no strings attached, and the logical thing to do was to accept it.

In the same way, if a God of love does exist, the rational thing to do is to accept his love, to come to know him. Entering into that kind of a relationship will have a positive effect, but that does not make the person weaker or somehow inferior to anyone else.

In contrast to the implication that those who need God are somehow inferior specimens of the human race is the Christian belief that there is an essential equality within humanity—all humans are precious beings who have been made in the image of God. At the same time, all humans are sinful and equally in need of God.

Freud did not really take issue with this idea of human fallibility; in fact, he believed in the reality of shame and guilt. Yet in his closed universe, with no ultimate authority, he struggled to deal with good and evil. As a consequence, he looked to the ideal of education as the solution. People must be taught that ethical behavior is in their own best interest, he stated; once they became well educated, they would naturally behave ethically. But can we really be sure that education in and of itself necessarily produces goodness? As one scholar notes, "Freud wrote this in 1927 before the Nazi rise in educated Germany."[18]

Yet even before that—as far back as 1913—Freud confessed to a friend, "That psychoanalysis has not made the analysts themselves better, nobler, or of stronger character remains a disappointment to me."[19]

The idea that Christianity is a crutch for weak people assumes that God is a human invention, that he is a psychological projection. We have seen that this argument cuts both ways as it could equally be argued that atheism is a psychological phenomenon and so it is nullified as a reasonable basis for rejecting God. The idea also assumes that belief in God provides people with a "crutch" and should be regarded with suspicion. Here we saw that something working ought not be a reason for rejecting it. On the contrary, if God does exist, we should surely expect his existence to have a real palpable impact on our lives.

As C. S. Lewis put it, "We may ignore, but we can nowhere evade, the presence of God. The world is crowded with Him."[20] To enter into a relationship with God is a logical response if he actually exists and reveals himself to people. It is only if he is not real that we ought to be worried about the "crutch" he provides.

And finally, we saw that we do not necessarily need to be weaker than or inferior to others if we accept God's offer of relationship and become Christians. In fact, it is the logical, reasonable response if God himself is real.

4

How Can You Say You Have Found the Truth If You Haven't Tried All the Alternatives?

A few years ago, I traveled through China with a group of friends. This beautiful country is so vast that it took us days of sitting on trains to get from one city to the next. As we got further north and west on our journey, the peppers in the food we ordered appeared smaller and smaller, eventually becoming tiny, very hot chili peppers. By the time we arrived in northwest China, the staple food had changed from rice to naan bread. I remember reflecting on how vast and diverse this country is as we sat for hours on end in third-class carriages accurately called "hard seat" in our guidebook.

Yet as diverse and huge as China is as a nation, it is but one nation of the world. Billions more people exist. In 2007 the estimated population of the world was 6.6 billion. That's a big number! It's hard to get your head around such a huge number of people. Add to this the myriad of different languages spoken; depending on how a language is defined there are estimated to be between four thousand and six thousand languages spoken in the world.

It is easy to see why so many people believe that there cannot be just one religion that is true for everyone in the world. The diverse cultures, colors and beliefs of the different people on this planet surely could not conform to one religious view, could they? Isn't the Christian one-size-fits-all approach to truth a colonial hangover that should not be taken seriously today?

It is intriguing that such an objection to truth is primarily leveled against religious belief rather than any other sphere of knowledge. Presumably it is not colonial to argue that global warming is a serious issue facing the planet and that this is true regardless of one's culture, color or language. Neither is it a naive one-size-fits-all approach to argue that historical events such as the First World War or the killing fields of Cambodia actually happened and have helped shape the present time.

Truth can be truth in a global sense as long as religion is kept out of things, it seems. But for the Christian, this assumption that "religion" is in a separate category from knowledge, fact, science and philosophy is an assumption that must be challenged. Where has this separation come from?

LOGICAL POSITIVISM

Logical positivism can be characterized by just one key idea: the verification principle. It states that a proposition can be "cognitively meaningful" only if there is a finite procedure for determining whether it is true or false. Consequentially, meta-physical, theological and ethical statements fall short of this criterion and so cannot be meaningful. This school of thought was developed by a group of philosophers called the Vienna Circle as well as by British philosophers like A. J. Ayer.

Critics of this philosophy have pointed out that logical posi-tivism's tenets cannot themselves be formulated in a way that is self-consistent and that the verification principle is not itself verifiable. In other words, this philosophy fails its own test.

Despite such an obvious flaw, logical positivism has im-pacted the public consciousness and influenced many people to suspect that ethical or theological propositions and con-siderations should not be articulated in the public sphere. An example of this is David Pannick QC, top U.K. barrister and human rights expert for the London-based British newspaper *The Times;* he commented on human rights legislation: "Reli-gious principles are based on sincere beliefs for which there is neither a rational basis nor empirical evidence. The legislative process demands stricter standards of scrutiny. . . . Parliament legislates by reference to rational analysis and not dogma."[1]

In spite of this suspicion of metaphysics and theology, the positive outcomes of the Christian worldview are still consid-ered desirable within society, even to those who reject the basis of these virtues as unfactual or irrational. Theologian Lesslie Newbigin writes,

> Middle class parents want values to be taught to children in schools because life will be more pleasant if these val-ues are adhered to. But they do not ask whether these values have any relations to the "facts" as taught in

school. They do not ask whether it is possible to believe that concern for minorities, for the poor, for the disabled is important if the fact is that human life is the result of the success of the strong eliminating the weak. If it is a "fact" that human life is the accidental result of the ruthless suppression of the weak by the strong and it is not a fact that "Man's chief end is to glorify God and enjoy him forever," then "values" have no factual basis. They can only be the expression of what some people choose, and inevitably it will be the strong who prevail. . . . We cannot use the language of right and wrong because it has no basis in "facts" as we understand them.[2]

Here we see that metaphysical values do play a real part in our society and legislatures, and yet the basis for this is not questioned. Logical positivism can offer no rationale for such values.

SEARCHING FOR TRUTH

While logical positivism stumbles over the hurdle of self-consistency, is it possible to look deeper than the attractive values or virtues of Christianity and establish the truthfulness of its foundations? Lesslie Newbigin offers three useful observations about truth.

The first token of reality is a *sense of meaning*. When a scientist struggles to make sense of a whole lot of apparently random data, and suddenly sees a picture that holds it all together, then the conviction occurs that something true has been discovered. The sense of meaning and beauty, of symmetry and coherence—these are the first tests of objectivity. The second test, of course, is that the scientist publishes these findings and invites other scientists to *consider their worth*—their truth. This is relevant to the whole question of Christian mission and evangelism. . . . Thirdly *if something is true it will lead to further truths.*[3]

Christian truth stands or falls like any other form of presupposition, philosophy or debate and thus contends in the public sphere with other ideas, be they Marxist, naturalist, Buddhist or any other worldview. It should not be confined to a religious sphere where meaning and reality are of a different order from the rest of the "real" world. The scale and use of numbers—the billions of people and thousands of languages in the world—is not the deciding factor as to whether Christianity is true or not.

This idea that one religion cannot be a fit for everyone also reveals the questioner's perspective on what the religions of the world actually are. Of course one can see quite clearly that if humanity is reaching out for God and trying to find him, then lots of pathways would need to be constructed, representing the diversity of the humans they were made for. But this goes precisely against what the Christians claim, namely that humans do not need to construct a pathway to God but rather that God has made the path himself. Jesus claims to be God in human form, a divine initiative to reconcile a broken world to God, not a man-made road of discovery to find God.

This divine initiative is God revealing himself to the whole world—no human attempt at discovery could come close to this. The earliest activity of the church reveals a community without walls; beginning in the Middle East, the church grew in Africa, Asia and Europe and only much later in the Americas and Australasia. The reality of God revealed in Christ is relevant to the whole world. Christianity presents a universal truth claim that can authentically unite and mix together different communities, ethnicities and *people* rather than trying to mix together a hodgepodge of *ideas*.

INTOLERANCE

But if we challenge the downgrading of Christian truth from the public to the "religious" sphere, it is still difficult to present Christ as uniquely true in our postmodern society. This is because it sounds intolerant and arrogant to say that Jesus is the only way to God. As we have already seen, *tolerance* can be defined as "the willingness to accept or tolerate somebody or something, especially opinions or behavior that you may not agree with, or people who are not like you." The ironic thing here is that for tolerance to be real, the integrity of different belief systems and cultures must be maintained. And yet Western culture constantly seeks to homogenize all the world's religions as either equally true or equally irrelevant on the basis that people are genuine in their beliefs.

In the successful novel *Chocolat*, which was made into a Hollywood blockbuster, the main character typifies this approach:

All stories delighted [my mother]—Jesus and Eostre and Ali Baba working the homespun of folklore into the bright fabric of belief again and again. Crystal healing and astral projection, abductions by aliens and spontaneous combustions, my mother believed them all. Or pretended to believe.

Later on in the book, someone asks the main character, "And what if it isn't an impertinent question—what do you believe?"

Magic carpet rides, rune magic, Ali Baba and visions of the Holy Mother, astral travel and the future in the dregs of red wine. . . . Buddha. Frodo's journey into Mordor. The transubstantiation of the sacrament. Dorothy and Toto. The Easter bunny. Space aliens. The Thing in the closet. The Resurrection and the Life at the turn of a card. . . . I've believed them all.[4]

This fictional character believes that all the religions and superstitions of the world are on the same level—Jesus and space aliens, Buddha and the Easter bunny. Yet doesn't this exactly mirror what so many people believe tolerance is? John Hick, Emeritus Danforth Professor of the Philosophy of Religion, Claremont Graduate University, California, summarizes the absurdity of this popular view: "To say that whatever is sincerely believed, and practised is, by definition, true, would be the end of all critical discrimination, both intellectual and moral."[5]

AN ACCIDENT OF BIRTH

Alongside these questions of truth and toleration is the underlying assumption that one's religion is completely determined by the circumstances of one's birth. And so the logic goes: an Indian is likely to be a Hindu; an Arab is likely to be a Muslim. On account of this observation, it is argued, all religions must be equal paths to the truth. But this makes truth a function of birth. If I were to be born into Communist North Korea, I would likely be a Communist—but does this make Communism true? No other intellectual discipline would accept such a superficial approach to truth. Why accept it here, when it comes to a fundamental belief system?

But more important, notice the arrogance of the assumption: you as a Christian are biased by the circumstances of your life, but I as a skeptic am completely neutral in my thinking. Isn't it just as likely that the secular thinking of the questioner has been passed on by the environment of the person and is culturally conditioned? In fact, the assumption that Christianity is a Western religion and that you believe it because you were raised in the church could not be further from the truth. The average Anglican in the world is a female black African under thirty years old. This dispels the white-male, middle-aged misconceptions of the church that many people labor beneath. In fact, the declining numbers in church attendance in Britain make it countercultural for anyone in that society to be a thoughtful Christian. While all around the world, whether in China, rural India or sub-Saharan Africa, Christianity grows and spreads like wildfire.

But this brings us back to the original question: "How can you claim to know the truth if you haven't tried all the alternatives?" Although this question may sound like a desire to engage in the search, it may actually be a complete shutdown, a dead end, because at the heart of this statement is the idea that, ultimately, truth is unknowable, since it would not be humanly possible to exhaustively look into all the alternatives. It is the ultimate excuse to stop bothering to look.

It may be helpful to imagine for a moment that instead of talking about God we are talking about the existence of something simpler, for example, a purple fish. To answer the question "Do purple fish exist?" I would have to conduct a search of the world or even the universe until I found a purple fish. Once I have found the fish, I would not need to go on searching in order to know it exists, because I have found the answer. The same is true with relationship with God through Christ. I conduct a search, I encounter the truth in Christ, and I do not need to go on looking elsewhere, since I have found what I was looking for.

An Indian friend of mine had been struggling for a long time with suicidal thoughts; he was extremely depressed and found himself unable to muster the energy to work or to devote proper time to his family. In his desperation, he went to visit a Hindu guru, wondering if this wise old man might be able to help him. Having poured out his troubles to this man, he asked, "Can you help me?"

The guru replied, "I cannot. There is only one person who has ever had any success in cases like this that I know of."

My friend pressed him, "Tell me who this is so that I can go to him."

The guru replied, "He is Jesus Christ."

My friend asked, "Where can I find this Jesus Christ?" The guru explained that he would need to read the Bible and that he should try a local church. As a result of that encounter, my friend came to Christ for himself. He knew something of the competing claims of Hinduism and Islam, although he was by no means a scholar, yet he was able to encounter the truth of Christ and realize that he had in one sense completed his journey but that in another it was only just beginning.

A part of the process of searching for the truth may involve looking comparatively at claims competing with those of Christ. Although not strictly necessary for everybody, it may help some to know what the different answers of different worldviews are to the same questions. As well as examining rival competing claims, it may be important to examine the evidence for the claim being made, be it historical, philosophical, moral, scientific or existential. As a Christian, I would argue that the Christian worldview provides the most coherent and convincing explanation of reality.

Jesus himself encourages us to do this searching, saying, "Ask and it will be given to you; seek and you will find; knock and the door will be opened to you" (Matthew 7:7). Becoming a Christian is not a closing down of the mind; it is an encounter with the truth, unhindered by an accident of birth.

5

If Christianity Is About Relationship with God, Why Does He Let Bad Things Happen to His Friends?

As a young boy called Medad played in the dust of a Ugandan village outside his house, he heard his parents arguing. His brother and he were keeping out of the way, hoping not to be noticed by their angry father. "But we need some land to grow food!" Medad heard his mother's voice cry. "How can I feed the children with no land and no money?" They came out of the house—he with his things packed in a case, she wiping her tears with her apron. Medad watched as his father, with a look of angry determination, picked up a handful of dust, threw it into the air and cursed his own wife and children: "May you be like this dust—useless and worthless, scattered by the wind." With that he turned, and he was gone.

This man had sold everything the family had and was leaving them destitute to go and live with his younger wives elsewhere. This was senseless cruelty, and Medad could not understand how or why such a thing could happen.

Living in the world as it is, all of us feel this to one degree or another. It is a reality that unites all humans—grief and pain in the face of injustice and loss.

Why do bad things happen to good people? Whatever our background or culture, this is a universal question. The prophet Jeremiah said, "I would speak with you about your justice: Why does the way of the wicked prosper? Why do all the faithless live at ease?" (Jeremiah 12:1). And the psalmist wrote, "But as for me, my feet had almost slipped; I had nearly lost my foothold. For I envied the arrogant when I saw the prosperity of the wicked" (Psalm 73:2-3).

A few days after the tsunami of 2005, one of the tires on my car needed to be replaced, so my husband and I slowly drove to our local garage, which happened to be open during that holiday season. We do not have a bumper sticker or tell-tale fish symbol on our car, so the mechanic could not have known that we were followers of Jesus.[1] As soon as we got out of the car, a mechanic began work on our tire. He remarked, "Well, the tsunami—it shows God doesn't exist."

Hoping to be in and out as quickly as possible so that we could drive to see our family, my heart sank as I realized we were about to begin a conversation about God and suffering. This is never an easy or quick subject to discuss. Before we embarked on a longer conversation, I asked him, "You are saying that you don't believe in God because this terrible thing has happened. But did you believe in God when things were going well in your life?" We were there for quite a while longer than our car needed, discussing these heartfelt questions openly and honestly, exploring together what God might be like if he actually exists—all while the mechanic fixed our tire.

Questions around this theme come up time and time again. "If God is so good, how can we understand suffering—especially of good people?" It is crucially important that we engage with this question, because it drives at the very heart of whether Christianity is true and real.

The subject of suffering—particularly the suffering of the innocent—has engaged the thinking of the human race across the spectrum of worldviews since the beginning of time. Some have fatalistically reconciled themselves to this question of suffering, while others have used it to rule out the existence of a good God. Still others have concluded that suffering is the only universal reality that humans experience and that they seek release from it by attaining enlightenment of some kind. It is one of the most difficult questions that humans have ever tried to address in our history.

Before we go any further, it is important to realize the philosophical nature of the question. While for many of us this issue of suffering is primarily personal and existential, it is also rational. The suffering of "good" people is a commonly given reason for disbelief in a good God. Emotions and philosophy are a potent mix, and we need to be careful to give enough attention to these very different dimensions to the question of suffering. This is important because pain and suffering can only be deemed a "problem" at a philosophical level if God actually exists.

God's character and very existence are regularly being

called into question on the basis of the intuitive moral judgments humans make. But employing the reality of suffering in order to deny the existence of a good God is to make a moral judgment. Such a moral judgment requires an objective moral law in order to meaningfully contrast good and evil. Yet, if an objective moral law exists rather than the moral preferences of individuals or societies, by logical consequence there must be a moral lawgiver. This would be God. The problem of suffering (when raised as a disproof of God) assumes the reality of the God it is trying to disprove.

But if theism establishes an objective moral law and provides a frame of reference within which it is possible to discuss the reality and pain of suffering, we should be careful to remember that the issue of suffering must be faced by all worldviews, including the atheistic systems of thought. It is not only the Christian who must do this. The question to be asked is, which worldview adequately faces it and has the resources to handle it?

NATURALISM

Naturalism is a system of thought that holds that all phenomena can be explained in terms of natural causes and laws. This means that the physical universe as well as metaphysical constructs, such as moral or religious truths, are derived from natural causes and not from revelation.

Many naturalists deny the very existence of evil because, as we have seen, discussion of good and evil as real categories leads us down a road of postulating a moral lawgiver. The consistent naturalist cannot have moral absolutes in a godless universe, because without God, there is no basis for any absolute moral judgment. Richard Dawkins puts to us the naturalistic perspective:

> If the universe were just electrons and selfish genes, meaningless tragedies . . . are exactly what we should expect, along with equally meaningless good fortune. Such a universe would be neither evil nor good in intention. . . . In a universe of blind physical forces and genetic replication, some people are going to get hurt, other people are going to get lucky, and you won't find any rhyme or reason in it, nor any justice. The universe we observe has precisely the properties we should expect if there is, at bottom, no design, no purpose, no evil and no good, nothing but blind pitiless indifference.[2]

This fascinating paragraph articulates the naturalistic problem very well. But it also reveals some of the problems an atheistic outlook must deal with. Dawkins seeks to deny the existence of moral categories while at the same time using the very *same* moral categories in his arguments. The basic premise is that good and evil do not exist. Yet Dawkins refers to "good fortune," of a lack of "justice" and of "pitiless indifference." This reveals a common problem in the reasoning of atheist antagonists: they often want to deny the existence of God and of any absolute standards, yet they seek to employ moral categories at the very same time.

The problem is that we all intuitively know that some things really are right and others really are wrong. This goes beyond personal preference or culture and points to the existence of a moral law and ultimately to God, the moral lawgiver.

EASTERN PHILOSOPHY

A situation similar to that of naturalism arises in Eastern phil-osophy. Here any distinction between good and evil either does not exist or at the very least belongs to an illusory realm. Trying to make sense of suffering is in itself a failure to understand that suffering is an illusion. Pain or grief following loss and tragedy results from desiring something (*tanha* in Buddhism), and suffering is a consequence of failing to transcend one's own desires. One's so-called suffering really has no meaning, because it is all an illusion. Such a view in practice seeks to transcend or ignore the reality of suffering for the individual, but also fails to deal with a desire for justice against the perpetrator of evil.

During a debate, one noted Zen Buddhist scholar and chair of comparative religion, when asked about the morality of Hitler's gas chambers replied, "That was very *silly* of him."

"Not evil then?" came the response.

The scholar replied, "Evil is a Christian concept. . . . Thinking in opposite categories is alien to our thought."[3]

ISLAM

Islam is a deterministic worldview that teaches that a transcendent God directly controls the workings of every individual. Human beings do not have free will. There is only one will in the universe and that is Allah's will (*inshallah*).

The outworking of this can be surprising to experience. I recently met a British soldier who had been serving in Iraq, helping to train the Iraqi army. The recruits were doing a simple survival exercise that involved jumping into a swimming pool fully clothed and carrying a fully loaded backpack of gear and weapons, then swimming to the surface. Two Iraqis were to go first and demonstrate to the rest of the group the effort involved in swimming with such a great weight pulling them down. The first struggled to the surface relatively quickly; the second sank to the bottom of the pool and made no movement at all. He did not even attempt to swim to the top. The commanding officer dove in and rescued him, dragging him out of the pool and saving his life.

The British soldiers asked him afterward, "Why didn't you try to swim to the surface? You said you could swim."

He replied, "I can swim but I knew that everything is Allah's will. I determined that if he willed it, I would live. Since you rescued me, obviously he did will that I live."

The British soldiers were shocked by this answer, but it gives us a fascinating insight into the Islamic understanding of God. For the Muslim, God is not just in control of the universe, he is literally pulling all the strings, determining all the decisions that are made and bringing about his will in the world all the time.

Islam means submission or surrender to God's will. The goal of the Muslim is to submit to God's will and to bring others in the world into submission to that will. This means that since both good and evil exist, they must both be God's will. When Muhammad was asked about this by his followers, the Hadith records the incident,

> Abu Bakr asserts that "Allah decrees good but does not decree evil" but Umar says that "He decrees both alike." Muhammad replied to this: "The decree necessarily determines all that is good and all that is sweet and all that

is bitter, and that is my decision between you. . . . O Abu Bakr if Allah had not willed that there be disobedience, He would not have created the Devil."[4]

It follows then that for Muslims these kinds of questions about evil do not tend to be phrased in quite the same way, since it is clear that God's will is necessarily what happens and human beings ought to submit to this reality. We need to be careful not to be confused here; this is substantively different from Christian thought. Even a Christian theology with a strong focus on predestination factors in a place for the human will and certainly gives moral responsibility to the individual for the choices she or he makes.

CHRISTIANITY

The Bible does not deny the reality of evil and suffering as some might expect when they think of a sanitized, insipid, moralistic caricature of the church. The biblical worldview does not speak of an unreal world of saccharine sweetness and fluff. The pain of human experience is fully appreciated and explored in the text of the Bible. For example, we see frustration ("Why does the way of the wicked prosper?" Jeremiah 12:1); desperation over such painful experiences as childlessness ("Give me children, or I'll die!" Genesis 30:1); loneliness ("I am the only one left," 1 Kings 19:10); grief over war ("My eyes will flow unceasingly, without relief," Lamentations 3:49); tears at bereavement ("Jesus wept," John 11:35); suffering from ill health ("A woman was there who had been subject to bleeding for twelve years," Luke 8:43); and the rape and killing of innocent people. Suffering in the world is no surprise to the

Christian; it is powerfully portrayed in the Bible as a reality of human experience.

The Bible does not just describe the world as we know it; it also has explanatory power. The Bible talks of a good God creating a good world and specifically making creatures who have the capacity to love. We see that for love to exist, freedom must exist. If the humans God made were forced to love him and each other, they would not be human at all—they would be machines, and love would not truly exist. As C. S. Lewis wrote, "Free will, though it makes evil possible, is also the only thing that makes possible any love or goodness or joy worth having. A world of automata—of creatures that worked like machines—would hardly be worth creating."[5]

For love to exist, it must be freely given. But where does evil come from? Isn't it also a created entity, as Muslims claim. No. In the Bible, evil is a counterfeit; it is not part of creation. Lewis calls it "a parasite, not an original thing."[6] The devil was not created as evil; he is Lucifer, a good angel who is fallen.

An illustration may help us here. In order to make a room dark, we do not switch darkness *on*—we switch the light *off*. Darkness is a negative entity that can be explained only as the absence of light. So it is with evil. It is a subversion of good rather than a created entity itself. Because true holiness is love, it can operate only in an atmosphere of freedom. Thus morality as a function of freedom in finite creatures has to reckon with the possibility that good may fall and thus produce evil.

An infinitely moral, holy God placed his creation under the stewardship of human beings who were created by him to share his moral characteristics (see Genesis 1:26-28). It is because we have rebelled against God that we have fractured relationships—with ourselves, with others, with God and with nature. Evil is good that has fallen.

What is God's answer? Instead of destroying our freedom, he identifies with our suffering in the person of Jesus Christ. The cross is God's answer to a hurting world. We do not have a distant God who orders us around arbitrarily; rather we encounter a God who is willing to identify with us to such an extent that he takes the consequences of our sin and disobedience on himself without violating our freedom. We are free to return to him and find our fulfillment in relationship with him. He offers to forgive, cleanse and restore us through the cross. He takes the penalty of our sin and pays for it with his own blood. The cost of his love for us at the cross shows us the depth and reality of this love.

Christianity does claim to have the apparatus and framework to explain the existence of good and evil, but this is never to negate the deep, heartfelt questions that human pain and suffering inevitably leave us with. Sometimes these questions are too complex or mysterious for us to even voice, but other questions can be articulated and formed, and it is possible to begin to explore them from a Christian perspective.

IF I AM SUFFERING, IS IT BECAUSE I HAVE SINNED?

Is there a causal link between my sin and suffering? For a Christian, the answer is "not necessarily." We may have been sinned against and that causes our suffering. Yet if I have cancer, it doesn't mean that there is necessarily a causal link with a particular sin I have committed. The book of Job in the Old Testament tells the story of a man who loses everything—his family, his wealth and his health. He is a righteous man, but his friends assume that he must have sinned to deserve this state of affairs. God vindicates Job.

The Christian worldview explains the existence of evil in the world as a result of the Fall and is clear that this affects us all. Sometimes we will suffer, and there will be no direct reason for this other than our humanness and the fact that we live in a real, fallen world. We cannot draw a line too clearly between individual sin and suffering.

Hinduism does this with the law of karma, which has no parallel in the Christian worldview. Glenn Hoddle was the manager of the England football (soccer) team and, as such, his every move was scrutinized by the whole country. Hoddle made some famous comments explaining his beliefs in reincarnation and karma: "You and I have been physically given two hands and two legs and half-decent brains," he was quoted as saying. "Some people have not been born like that for a reason. The karma is working from another lifetime.

"I have nothing to hide about that. It is not only people with disabilities. What you sow, you have to reap."[7]

These comments caused an uproar, as the British public felt that a great injustice was being done to the disabled, and Hoddle was forced to resign.

The Old Testament book of Job reminds Christians that suffering is not due to karma or, necessarily, to sin. So does the New Testament and church history, since the apostles and many other wonderful Christians have suffered and died gruesomely. The psalmist continually asks questions as to why righteous people suffer. At least a part of the biblical answer is that this is a consequence of living in a fallen world as described for us in Genesis.

But suffering is more complex than this for the Christian, since it can be a direct consequence of sin, whether that be sinful abuse by another or our own fault. It may be that we suffer the consequences of our own folly when we contract cancer after smoking for years or end up alone after destroying our marriage by having an affair. Sometimes it is possible to see the reason for our suffering in our own actions.

More frequently we suffer at the hands of others. Living as I do in a deprived community of London, I encounter the horrific reality of this on a regular basis, whether it be domestic violence, rape, child abuse, contract killings, extortion or theft. All of these have been suffered by some in the congregation I am part of—suffering as the direct result of the evil in another person.

From a biblical perspective, this kind of suffering is put into an explanatory context by the beginning and the end of the Bible. In the beginning we see that a world in which love is possible entails human freedom. This choice is abused, and while love is possible, suffering also becomes part of the picture. However, the God who created the world will also judge the world, and so in the end, those who appear to get off scot-free in this life—abusing and violating others—will face the judgment of God. He will ensure that justice is done in the end.

Persecution. There are further reasons why Christians suffer, the most obvious of which is that they may be suffering for their faith. Persecution has been a constant companion for the follower of Jesus from the very earliest moments of the church to the present day. Today Christians suffer in China, the Middle East, Indonesia and elsewhere simply for believing in Jesus.

My colleague Michael Ramsden recently met a wonderful Christian in Indonesia. She had been attending a church service when militant Islamists[8] threw grenades into the building, killing some of the worshipers. As survivors ran out of the church, they were shot. One man got hold of this woman, put the barrel of the gun in her mouth, and commanded, "Renounce Jesus and live." She replied that she would not, that she loved and worshiped Jesus. He pulled the trigger. Half of her face was blown away but, amazingly, she survived. When Michael asked her what she felt about her oppressor, she said, "I must love and forgive as Jesus did." She now spends her time visiting homes in the community that the militants come from, sharing the message of God's love and serving in practical ways.

The promise of Jesus is "blessed are those who are persecuted" (Matthew 5:10). Suffering is not necessarily seen as an entirely negative thing in the Bible; it can even be a sign of God's favor. A number of years ago I visited China with a group of students, and we had the privilege of attending an underground church. The pastor of this church had spent nineteen years doing hard labor in a camp for his faith, and his church was continuously interrupted and raided by the police, who confiscated Bibles and destroyed equipment.

When we asked him what the secret of his church's growth was, he said without hesitation: "Persecution." We must have looked surprised, because he went on to explain, "Every time I am imprisoned or the building is raided, our church doubles in size again. When the police come and start harassing us, we know that good things are about to happen." This has been the story of the church throughout the ages; hence the often-quoted phrase "The blood of the martyrs is the seed of the church."[9] Historically, where Christians are persecuted, churches often grow and flourish.

Suffering in the cause of justice. It is also possible to suffer for working hard in the cause of his or her faith. It may not be persecution per se, but rather suffering in the cause of justice. William Wilberforce experienced this through exhaustion, discouragement and illness during his Bible-inspired campaign to see an end to slavery in the British Empire. The apostle Paul experienced similar suffering as he worked hard to preach and establish churches. Amy Carmichael experienced suffering as she established a loving home for hundreds of abused or orphaned Indian children. Suffering may well come if a Christian is working hard for the cause of Christ.

A time of trial. Christians also experience suffering that puts their faith through a time of trial, purifying motives and attitudes. Again, the New Testament writers expected Christians to experience many kinds of trials, including suffering in the body, which can be for our own good.

For example, we quickly learn as children not to touch hot things. The pain of burning is a good kind of pain, since it tells us to remove our hand from the fire. If this pain did not function, the hand could be completely destroyed. When a Christian suffers, it may be this kind of pain—pain that serves a positive purpose. C. S. Lewis writes of suffering having this possible positive dimension: "Suffering is not good in itself. What is good in any painful experience is, for the sufferer, his submission to the will of God, and, for the spectators, the compassion aroused and the acts of mercy to which it leads."[10]

He goes on to explain that this redemptive view of suffering can even apply to the person who has experienced evil at the hands of another:

> Now the fact that God can make complex good out of simple evil does not excuse—though by mercy it may save—those who do simple evil. And this distinction is central. Offences must come, but woe to those by whom they come; sins do cause grace to abound, but we must not make that an excuse for continuing to sin.[11]

In all of this we must remember that sufferers may not know at the time why they are suffering—whether simply in consequence of living in a fallen world or as a result specifically of their own sin, another's sin or persecution. We must also be careful not to assume we know the reason for someone else's suffering. Job's friends in the Old Testament were severely warned against pronouncing the reasons for suffering (Job 42:7).

WHY DOESN'T GOD ALWAYS INTERVENE?

The next obvious question then is, why doesn't God intervene on behalf of his followers in order to prevent or alleviate their suffering? We have already examined the positive role of suffering in the life of the believer, and so it may be for some higher, greater purpose that the Christian is allowed to go through the experience. But there is also a theological context that may help us to understand this from a biblical perspective, especially as God does *sometimes* intervene miraculously, delivering people from danger, disease or death. This can be called the "now and not yet" of the kingdom of God.

Jesus' coming to earth and leaving his followers with the Holy Spirit inaugurates his kingdom. And so he says, "The kingdom of God is within you" (Luke 17:21). This means that "the blind receive sight, . . . the good news is preached to the poor" (7:22). But the kingdom is also "coming"[12]—there is a future hope. When Jesus returns, there will be a final judgment and a new heaven and earth. This is when suffering finally ends. Miraculous interventions in the present are signs pointing toward this future reality. They are not deserved badges of God's favoritism for the individual who is healed or helped, but rather visible signs for everyone to see that this future judgment and bliss is really coming.

I remember visiting a member of our congregation in the hospital; he was dying of an aggressive cancer. He was a senior government official with a wonderful family and a strong Christian faith, and doing tremendous, meaningful work. As my husband and I went in to pray for him, he said, "A miracle is God's to give, not ours to take." This humble, godly man was given a further two years of life, against all medical prediction. He did have more work to do and then died peacefully with his family around him. That is a wonderful example of a Christian facing suffering, experiencing God's intervention and then having peace to face death.

Medad, the little Ugandan boy I began this chapter with, is a friend of mine today, forty years after that terrible experience when his father cursed the family and left. He grew up trying to scratch out a living, working as a child to put food in the mouths of his family. As a teenager, he became a Christian and sought to turn away from theft and fraud and to educate himself. Through determination and hard work, he succeeded to the point that he now has a doctorate. All of his family also became Christians, and they slowly but surely rebuilt their lives.

One day Medad was sitting with his mother when a voice they recognized came onto the radio. It was the man who had abandoned them so long ago. He was weak and dying, having fallen on hard times. Thrown out by the woman he had been living with, he made this appeal: "If any of my family hear this, please remember me and have pity on me." Medad's mother, now a Christian herself, took her husband back. She looked after him and cared for him, demonstrating God's love in action. She forgave him everything, even going on to have another child by him. This forgiving love, which he did not deserve, was an outpouring of her love for Jesus. Although she had suffered horrendously, God made something beautiful out of her life.

A Christian discussion of the question of suffering is not simplistic; neither does it claim to be comprehensive, because an element of mystery in the pain remains. However, it does engage with philosophical issues and is pragmatically realistic about the world. It goes beyond its rivals in its explanatory power, diagnosing the problem of evil and introducing us to a God who acts in the world, meeting us in our pain and dealing with our sin at the cross. The Bible engages with suffering as a reality, dealing with human moral responsibility but also introducing us to a God who enters into the suffering world and suffers himself on the cross to redeem humanity.

6

If Christianity Is About a Transforming Relationship with God, Why Are Christians So Bad?

When asked what one question about the Christian faith he found most difficult to answer, a Christian leader friend of mine responded, "If Christ transforms us, why do we see so little evidence of this in some of his followers?"

This is not to say that there aren't many wonderful individual Christians and communities of Christians out there demonstrating his transforming power, but rather that a widespread objection to the Christian faith is the type of life displayed by many Christians. The fact that this objection exists shows that onlookers believe an encounter with Christ should morally transform a person but that sometimes this simply doesn't seem to happen.

Bertrand Russell's daughter wrote,

I would have liked to convince my father that I had found what he had been looking for, the ineffable something he had longed for all his life. I would have liked to persuade him that the search for God does not have to be in vain. But it was hopeless. He had known too many blind Christians, bleak moralists who sucked the joy from life and persecuted their opponents; he would never have been able to see the truth they were hiding.[1]

I remember the cold sweat breaking out on my head and the sinking feeling in the pit in my stomach when I heard that a Christian leader who had been a good friend of ours had cheated on his wife. The devastation felt by his wife and children at this senseless betrayal was made all the more awful by the pain and disappointment felt by the many hundreds of members of the thriving church he had led. The newspaper headlines followed, and the critics smiled, reassured in their opinion that Christianity was impotent and empty, a useless religion for a bygone age, demanding moral standards that even its leaders were unable to live up to.

For some, this issue is simply an excuse to hide behind: "Christians are hypocrites, therefore I don't have to take the claims of Christ or the evidence for the truthfulness of Christianity seriously." The charge of hypocrisy is an interesting one, since the word *hypocrite* can mean "a person who acts in contradiction to his or her stated beliefs or feelings."[2] The question here is one of authenticity. If followers of Jesus contradict their beliefs with their actions, this undermines their integrity and not necessarily their stated beliefs. But *hypocrisy* is a useful word with which to keep an overenthusiastic Christian at bay.

For others, this question is personal, real and compelling. The victims of sexual abuse at the hands of a priest, the congregation of a charismatic pastor who turns out to be a philanderer, the neighbors of self-righteous and selfish churchgoers all produce disappointment with Christians, causing others to close their hearts to Christ.

The first thing I would say in response to this objection is that Christians are often the first to admit that we haven't got it all together—or at least we ought to be. When we do fail to live out our faith, we must recognize that this is a serious matter. However, this should not discourage a skeptic from at least taking a look first and foremost at Christ. I may not be the best example of a Christian, but please don't let that stop you from seeing Christ for yourself. The brilliant Russian writer Fyodor Dostoyevsky said, "I believe that there is no one deeper, lovelier, more sympathetic and more perfect than Jesus—not only is there no one else like him, there never could be anyone like him."[3]

Napoleon Bonaparte commented,

I know men and I tell you that Jesus Christ is no mere man. Between him and every other person in the world there is no possible term of comparison. Alexander, Caesar, Charlemagne and I founded empires. But on what did we rest the creations of our genius? Upon force. Jesus Christ founded his empire upon love, and at this hour millions of people would die for him.[4]

These are astounding words from a ruthless and brilliant world leader. But if Christ is magnetic, dynamic and perfect, what about his followers? It was Gandhi who once said, "I like

your Christ. I do not like your Christians. You Christians are
so unlike your Christ."[5] This disappointment with some of the
followers of Jesus points to the heart of the Christian faith.
Christians are not those who try to do good things but those
who have received forgiveness and grace from God in Christ
and are transformed by knowing him.

Christ came for imperfect people. Jesus said, "For I have
not come to call the righteous, but sinners" (Matthew 9:13). It
should not be surprising to us that Christians are not perfect,
since the heart of Jesus' message is our very need for forgiveness. This is the greatest attraction of the Christian gospel—
that we can come to Jesus in all our ugliness, impurity and
brokenness.

Many people think that being a Christian means being a
good person who tries hard and is a touch morally superior, but
nothing could be further from the truth. At the heart of Christianity is the offer of forgiveness, but we have to recognize our
own moral bankruptcy and our need for this forgiveness in
order to access it. This doesn't happen only at the beginning of
a relationship with God; in fact, the continuing journey of faith
involves a constant process of confessing our sins.

I love the words of the Anglican prayer book, which are
taken from 1 John 1:8. I remember hearing these words every
week as a child: "If we claim to be without sin, we deceive
ourselves and the truth is not in us. If we confess our sins, he
is faithful and just and will forgive us our sins and purify us
from all unrighteousness."

If Christianity is, at its center, the offer of forgiveness, it
should not be surprising that broken people take it up and,
during the process of transformation by Christ, hardly shine

as examples of "good" people. A helpful question may be asked here though: What would the life of the individual in question have been like without his or her faith in Christ. Even if this person is not an amazing saint, has his or her life since encountering Christ changed trajectory?

In my church in Peckham, which is inner-city London, a group of young gang members told my husband, the vicar, that, since they had committed their lives to God earlier that week, they had decided to become a Christian gang called "the Christian gangstas." He looked a little uncomfortable, trying not to imagine the headlines: "Church gang attacks man." He asked them to tell him a little more. They said, "Because we're Christians and we believe in Jesus and the resurrection and all that yeah . . . we've decided we're not going to have guns." He felt pride swelling in his chest before they added, "Only knives, because you've got to protect yourself."

For them, discipleship was a process of giving up guns, then knives, then blunt instruments, then finally violence altogether. If all Christians were judged on the basis of someone meeting one of these guys while he still carried a blunt instrument, they might write Christianity off as violent. But the work of God in the gang members' lives was only beginning; these were major steps of discipleship for these young men. Now, some of them chose not to follow through as Christians, but others have become passionate followers of Christ, shining as examples of wonderful saints in a dark world.

If becoming a Christian has made no difference at all, then we must question the genuineness of the individual's faith. The apostle John certainly does this: "The man who says, 'I know him' but does not do what he commands is a liar, and the truth is not in him. But if anyone obeys his word, God's love is truly made complete in him" (1 John 2:4). Jesus was very harsh about people who claimed to be religious yet whose hearts and lives didn't match up to their outward projections (see Mark 12:38-40). He certainly taught that not everyone who claimed to be his follower actually was: "Not everyone who says to me, 'Lord Lord,' will enter the kingdom of heaven, but only he who does the will of my Father who is in heaven" (Matthew 7:21). This is a clear call for authenticity, as well as a timely reminder that we cannot always judge who is and who isn't a Christian.

When you see Christians who appear to be hypocrites, who are causing you to reject the gospel because of their lives, there are a number of possibilities. The first is that they have come into a relationship with God but are only at the beginning of the process of transformation. Changes are happening, but the brokenness is still all too evident.

The second are Christians who have been following Jesus and experiencing life-transforming power on the journey but then have had a spectacular slip-up. They let a lot of people down, including themselves. This happens in the Bible and does not completely nullify the individual if he or she comes to repentance and seeks restoration. King David committed adultery and murder in the Old Testament, and Peter denied Jesus in the New Testament. Both suffered serious consequences but were able to be forgiven and restored.

A third possibility are those who are not true followers of Jesus at all; their actions, attitudes, desires and words reveal what is in their hearts. They consistently live in a way that is contrary to Jesus' teaching, and there is no evidence whatsoever of his work in their lives.

I have a friend who became a Christian in college. He was passionate about his Christian faith and, one evening, invited his university and work colleagues to come and hear what had happened to him. One of his closest friends, the colleague he shared an office with, refused to come. My friend was hurt and disappointed, and so he asked this man why. He replied that he would not take the Christian message seriously because he had looked on while a woman claiming to be a Christian married his brother and then left him for someone else. Having cheated on him, she took this man's children away, devastating the whole family while claiming to be a follower of Jesus. The pain of all this was so great that—whatever Jesus' statements about adultery in the Bible—this man rejected Christianity for his brother's sake.

WHY DO CHRISTIANS SOMETIMES FAIL SO SPECTACULARLY?

We should not be taken by surprise when Christians, including leaders, fail. The Bible is not at all sycophantic about the people it introduces us to. The human failings of the prophets and apostles of the Scriptures are laid bare for all to see. In fact, it can be quite surprising to read statements made about the twelve disciples, such as "Jesus turned and rebuked them" (Luke 9:55) or "When Jesus saw this, he was indignant" (Mark 10:14)—a description of his response to the disciples after they tried to prevent children from coming to him. The human frailty of followers of Jesus, including leaders, is never underestimated in the biblical worldview. For instance, Paul rebuked the Corinthian church for having a bun fight and getting drunk during Holy Communion together. This inclusion in the New Testament reminds us of the nature of humanity.

When Christians fail spectacularly, it is human weakness reasserting itself. The reality of God's transforming power is all the more necessary when the raw material of human lives is examined. The church is made of broken people on a journey to wholeness; perfection is not expected overnight, but transformation of lives will be happening where Christ is genuinely at work.

Before my husband powerfully encountered God, he used a lot of bad language. Every other word was a swear word. He had tried to stop, but nothing worked. He just couldn't help it. After encountering Christ, his swearing stopped overnight. We have now been married for ten years, and I have never heard him swear. There were other areas in his life that took much longer to get sorted out, and some are yet to be dealt with, but this only goes to underline the ongoing reality of God's transforming power in a life.

The French mathematician and philosopher Blaise Pascal put it like this:

> For the Christian faith consists almost wholly in establishing two things: The corruption of nature and the redemption of Christ. Now I maintain that, if they do not serve to prove the truth of the redemption by the sanctity of their conduct, they do at least admirably serve to prove the corruption of nature.[6]

WHAT DOES MY LIFE SAY ABOUT ME?

"Actions speak louder than words." This is true whatever our worldview; the way we chose to live and the priorities we make reveal the true nature of our beliefs and values. For the Christian, this is challenging because Jesus' expectation is that his followers' lives would point to him. He said, "Let your light shine before men, that they may see your good deeds and praise your Father in heaven" (Matthew 5:16). He also warned that following him would entail cost and self-sacrifice: "If anyone would come after me, he must deny himself and take up his cross and follow me" (Luke 9:23). But the added complication for the Christian is that it isn't a simple case of humans trying hard to do these things on their own. Many people shrink back from starting to follow Jesus because they feel "I'm not good enough" or "I'm not going to be able to keep it up." But the promise of the Bible is that God will work in us, be with us and forgive us when we need it.

Although disappointing people who claim to be Christians are around, causing some to question the existence of God and his transforming power, many good, local, redemptive Christian communities do demonstrate the love, power and reality of God. I have personal experience of such Christian churches, sometimes meeting in affluent areas and sometimes gathering in places of desperation and even persecution.

A local politician recently visited a church in London. He had been impressed by the social justice and community projects the church was running. He had heard that violent criminals were changing, and he was intrigued. After experiencing one of the worship services, which he found "rather unnerving" due to the electric atmosphere, he asked to meet with the vicar. They went for a drink together, and the politician commented, "This church seems to be the only place where the cross-section of the community comes together—black and white, African and Caribbean, young and old, educated and illiterate, powerful and disenfranchised."

He went on. "If I go into a local pub, it will be for either white or black, either middle-class educated or manual workers. It is in the church that everyone comes together. If only it weren't for all the talk about God and Jesus, it would be fantastic. I'd be there every week." The leader of that church pointed out that it was precisely because of Jesus that this was possible; only because of him could people who have absolutely nothing else in common come together and have a shared identity.

This is the power of churches that have thoughtful theological convictions and are Spirit-empowered, worshiping, evangelizing, compassionate, serving communities. These churches may not be famous or slick, but they are all over the place, introducing people to Jesus, bringing his love and justice to the communities they serve and worshiping him together in unity.

As I travel to the different continents, I have had the privilege of meeting Christians living in many different circumstances. Sometimes they are working in conditions of appalling material poverty and sometimes they are living out their faith despite the oppression of the state. In these places of desolation, it is not unusual to find loving, committed, active Christian churches.

We should not be too quick to write off churches as hypocritical or failing in some way before examining our own hearts and motives. It was the great London preacher Charles Spurgeon who is reported to have said, "If you find the perfect church, don't join; you'll only spoil it!"

7

If God Is So Loving And Relational, Why Did He Go Ahead and Create When He Knew People Would End Up in Hell?

In our twenty-first-century sophistication, the idea of hell has become increasingly remote. Whether it be because of fifteenth-century portrayals of suffering illustrated with goblins and devils or because of twenty-first-century comedy in the form of cartoons such as *The Simpsons*, hell is not taken seriously by many people. I recently passed a car with this message in the window: "You say I'm going to Hell? That's where the party will be happening with all my friends. Bring it on." Jean-Paul Sartre wrote of hell as being "locked forever in a small room with two other people."[1] Woody Allen quipped, "Eternal nothingness is OK if you're dressed for it."[2]

The incredulity with which the Christian doctrine of hell

is met can be illustrated by the headlines that followed Pope Benedict's sermon about hell. He said, "Hell really exists and is eternal even if nobody talks about it much anymore." The shock of this, that a Christian leader actually believed in hell, prompted breathtaking headlines like "Pope Proclaims Hell Exists" in the *New York Post*[3] and "The Fires of Hell Are Real and Eternal, Pope Warns" in *The Times* (London).[4]

I was recently asked by an anxious student at Bristol University about hell. We had discussed the possibility of judgment, and I had explained something of the Christian perspective. She was quite agitated at the possibility of being held to account after death for actions in this life and kept insisting that there was no afterlife. When I said, "If you're so sure about that, you've got nothing to worry about, have you?" she began to press me for evidence supporting the Christian claims.

Such discussions of hell illustrate the importance of basing one's beliefs on truth and reality rather than on personal preference. If eternal life is at stake, isn't it at least worth examining the claims and teachings of Jesus and making up our minds properly about their veracity, rather than drifting along with society's laissez-faire attitude, hoping it will all pan out in the end?

Having negotiated one's way through the haze of humor and bemusement about the idea of hell, we are left with a number of serious questions to address. The first is, "If God is a loving God, why did he go ahead and create if he knew people would end up in hell?" The emotive force of this question makes it very powerful—surely if God really cared about people, it would be better not to have made them if he knew full well that many would enter an eternal destiny of suffering. The problem with the question is that it assumes that it is possible to make a like-for-like comparison between existence and nonexistence, and then go on to conclude that one is preferable or "better" than the other. But of course we as existing beings cannot possibly conceive of nonexistence in this way. As C. S. Lewis so eloquently put it,

> I must warn the reader that I shall not attempt to prove that to create was better than not to create: I am aware of no human scales in which such a portentous question can be weighed. Some comparison between one state of being and another can be made, but the attempt to compare being and not being ends in mere words. "It would be better for me not to exist"—in what sense "for me"? How should I, if I did not exist, profit by not existing?[5]

If we cannot compare being and nonbeing in this way, we can still question the character of God with regard to hell. Is it really part of the profile of a loving God to punish people?

JUSTICE AND JUDGMENT

I was driving home with my family from a wonderful skiing holiday in the French Alps a few weeks ago. My baby twin boys were gurgling in their car seats, our car was whizzing along the French autoroute, and we were listening to music when a police car began flashing its lights at us. In ten years of driving, I can honestly say that we had never been pulled over by the police, so we were quite surprised. We complied with their tactics and came to a stop.

We were informed that we had been speeding and that we now owed ninety euros. On top of all the toll charges in France, this felt like a lot of money, and I was furious. When we asked for evidence of our speeding, it emerged that my husband had gone over the limit by five kilometers per hour. "It's because we're English they are picking on us," I whispered to him.

We tried to be charming and say that we wouldn't do it again. We asked them to send us the ticket and evidence in the mail, as happens in the United Kingdom. But the wheels of bureaucracy had started to turn. The policeman threatened to impound our car unless we handed over the money there and then. He would not budge. We had no choice; we had to give him the precious notes we had saved for tolls. As we drove away, it slowly dawned on me that although I felt aggrieved at this injustice, we had actually broken the law, albeit by a tiny fraction. Justice had been done.

How we feel about justice depends on which side of the law we find ourselves on. Most people want to live in a society where there is a legal system that is just and fairly administered. When we are the victim of a crime, we long for justice to be meted out. If they really care for us, our loved ones want justice on our behalf too. Love and justice hold together. It would not be truly loving to ignore evil or injustice, so a loving God must also be a just God.

A friend of mine was recently beaten black and blue by her partner while her young children looked on. This man hit my friend so hard that she could not open one of her eyes for a day, and the doctors were concerned that her sight may have been permanently damaged. Covered in cuts and bruises, she went to the hospital but was unwilling to report the man to the police.

As her friend, my heart cried out for justice for her and her children. This is because I love her. Love and justice are close companions. We see this in the Bible. As my colleague Michael Ramsden often says, "The problem of evil is the problem of love." If love is to exist, it must be freely given and received—or else it is not love. If this freedom is possible, the withholding of love is possible. Selfishness, violence, injustice follow the abuse of love's freedom. A loving God cannot ignore these violations of his world; if he did, he would not truly be loving. This is where hell fits in—it is the means of God's judgment, allowing his justice to be upheld.

RETRIBUTION AND REVENGE

But why does God's judgment have to involve ideas of retribution and punishment in hell? Isn't this an outmoded and vindictive formula? Isn't it actually irreconcilable with a God of love? Isn't a vengeful God rather petty?

In fact, retribution is an important factor here because it connects the punishment with the sin in a real sense. It means that punishment is not arbitrary or random, but rational and consequential. If one of my boys hits his brother over the head and then bites his leg, he knows that he will be removed from the room where his toys and family are and placed in a corner of the hall for a period of time-out. He endures this separation for a minute or so if he has acted aggressively. Even as a toddler he understands that his action leads to punishment.

Wrongdoing must be recognized as such by both the perpetrator and the world around. That is the function of punishment. Not that petty rivalries and scores are settled in revenge but rather that justice requires that when a line is crossed, consequences follow. Hell is the ultimate degree of this; it is the destination of those who refuse to recognize their own sin for what it is, whose assertion of the self over others and God defies divine justice. Hell is the ultimate consequence of egoism.

IS HELL DISPROPORTIONATE?

Even if the idea of divine justice is upheld as consistent with a loving God, can eternal damnation of a human soul really be counted as a proportionate consequence for the sinner? This question often stems from the idea that the experience of hell is identical for mass murderers as for selfish egotists. But the Christian worldview allows for different experiences of hell that result directly from what an individual has thought, said and done in life.

Suffering in hell is directly related to the way that life has been lived on earth. For example, Jesus comments that religious hypocrites who oppress the disadvantaged will be "punished most severely" (Mark 12:40). Not everyone will receive the same punishment in hell or, for that matter, reward in heaven. What we do with our lives and with the opportunities we have been given will be reflected in our lives beyond the grave.

Thomas Aquinas answered objections that hell was a disproportionately harsh punishment for human sin by arguing that an offense against God is an offense against an infinite being and so, although the act itself is temporal and finite, its object is not. This means that the consequences reflect the nature of the recipient of the offense: "The magnitude of the punishment matches the magnitude of the sin. . . . God is of infinite greatness. Therefore an infinite punishment is deserved for a sin committed against him."[6]

The idea of eternal suffering as a result of temporal sinning is seen as disproportionate if the seriousness of sin is not fully appreciated. But a biblical view of sin positions it as crucially serious. We see two broad concepts that help us to define sin. The first is *transgression*, which means "to step across" or "go beyond a boundary." This very much carries the sense of breaking the law. The second is the idea of "missing the mark," which has connotations of a standard of perfection like a bull's-eye that we aim at but miss. The worth of each and every human being—created as we are in the divine image and given the capacity and opportunity to make choices—means that it is a serious thing to abuse this human dignity, whether by crossing the line or missing the mark. This applies to one's own life, to others and ultimately to defying the Maker himself.

The seriousness of sin in the Christian worldview is underscored further by the cost Jesus paid to deal with it. Unfortunately our familiarity with the cross of Jesus can obscure the wonder of the Christian message. I remember talking to a girl in Ireland after I had given a lecture at Galway University and taken questions from the students. She had grown up in a nominally Roman Catholic home and had walked past a crucifix hanging in her parents' hallway many hundreds of times. As we talked about the Christian view of what had happened at Christ's cross, her eyes filled with tears, and she remarked, "I never knew what it was about; it was just there, and I ignored it."

But the profundity of what happens at the cross and the suffering of God himself on our behalf bring the seriousness of our human predicament without Christ into sharp relief and throw some light on the nature of hell, from which we can be rescued. The cross is no easy thing. In the Bible we find many different images and analogies that reveal the full significance of the cross to us.

Sacrifice. Jesus' sacrifice for sin is explored for us using various images. *Expiation* means that the pure, holy Son of God takes the sin of the world on himself and bears it. This is no simple thing. Paul writes that God made "him who had no sin to be sin for us" (2 Corinthians 5:21). That means that Jesus, having lived a perfect life, knew sin only as something external to him that he observed, took sin into himself at the cross. Because Jesus was more than an ordinary man—he is God made flesh—he had the capacity to do this. He took the sins of the world on his shoulders.

But the sacrifice did not end there. *Propitiation* means that the punishment and wrath of God, the righteous judge against the evil of the world, are also poured out on Jesus. Divine justice is meted out upon sin, and Christ bore both the sin and its just consequences. He took our sin and the shame of our sin onto himself.

Christus Victor. Jesus made a famous statement from the cross: "It is finished." The sacrifice was made, and this signified that Jesus triumphed over evil, defeating the power of death. He is victorious over all darkness, sin, evil and injustice. For those trusting in Jesus, there is no need to worry that the punishment for sin will apply to them eternally.

Ransom. One of the key biblical images of sin is that of a slave master. As the United Kingdom celebrates the two hundredth anniversary of the abolition of the slave trade in the British Empire, this image is poignant today. The trafficking of human life, the shackling of people in iron and the branding of their skin, the physical pain and exhaustion suffered by men, women and children at the hands of their "owners," eventually caused outrage in Britain through the campaign of people like William Wilberforce. Slavery is the image that the biblical writers chose to use to explain the power of the cross of Christ to us. Jesus sets us—the slaves to sin—free. He ransoms us, delivering us from the hell of slavery.

Justification. Another powerful biblical image is that of the law court. Justice declares its verdict over our lives: we are not perfect; we are, in fact, guilty. There are consequences to be borne and justice must be upheld. At the cross, Christ bears those consequences for us and is able to forgive us our sins while still upholding justice. Because of the cross, the legally guilty are declared righteous.

All this demonstrates how serious sin is, since God himself paid such a price. The cross means that no one has to end up in hell and that forgiveness is offered to all. But forgiveness must be received, and for this a recognition of sin is essential. C. S. Lewis writes, "But forgiveness needs to be accepted as well as offered if it is to be complete: and a man who admits no guilt can accept no forgiveness."[7]

The astonishing thing in the Christian worldview is that God, who loves the world, shows mercy by coming into the world that he made, and he pays the price of the cross—and still people end up in hell. God does give us a way out—the chance to avoid hell—but he does it in a way that dignifies us as humans without overwhelming our will and undermining our essential being.

In the long run the answer to all those who object to the doctrine of hell, is itself a question: "What are you asking

God to do?" To wipe out their past sins and, at all costs, to give them a fresh start, smoothing every difficulty and offering every miraculous help? But He has done so, on Calvary. To forgive them? They will not be forgiven. To leave them alone? Alas, I am afraid that is what He does.[8]

8

Belief in God Is Dangerous

As the atheist cause proves less successful in convincing the wider population that God does not exist, the grounds for debate have slowly but surely shifted away from a simple theism/atheism debate toward portraying belief in God as dangerous—even evil. It was Woody Allen who commented, "And if it turns out that there is a God, I don't believe that he is evil. The worst that can be said is that he's an underachiever."[1] But nevertheless, a groundswell of articles and comments questioning the moral, political, psychological and intellectual safety of belief in God has been gathering momentum in the last few years.

WHAT KIND OF GOD DON'T YOU BELIEVE IN?

A few years ago a friend from university days at Oxford was working in a large company, having graduated with a top degree. Miles wanted to share his faith in Christ with his work colleagues but found that opportunities to talk about the deep questions of life were quite few and far between. One friend in particular was fairly hostile toward any mention of God, so Miles asked him, "What kind of a God don't you believe in?" When his friend described God to him, Miles was able to say, "I don't believe in that God either. Let me tell you what I do believe in."

Richard Dawkins is an eloquent preacher of secularism who describes God as "a petty, unjust, unforgiving control freak; a vindictive, bloodthirsty ethnic cleanser; a misogynistic, homophobic, racist, infanticidal, genocidal, filicidal, pestilential, megalomaniacal, sadomasochistic, capriciously malevolent bully."[2] It is hardly surprising that he rejects God as an invented "delinquent." God, it seems, is provoking more vociferous debate today about his nature and character than about his existence.

This is an interesting development and provides the Christian with an opportunity to talk about the being of God from a biblical perspective. For the Christian, the supreme revelation of God is in his incarnation. The person of Christ reveals God to us. Christ shows us God as Father—encouraging us to refer to God using *Abba*, a beautifully intimate Aramaic word for "father." Jesus shows us that God is compassionate and concerned with the plight of the poor and broken. Christ reveals God as the self-sacrificing Judge—the one who upholds justice and mercy, supremely through the cross.

To dismiss God on the basis of a flagrant misrepresentation of his character is shallow beyond belief. As Alister McGrath writes of Dawkins's God, "Come to think of it, I don't believe in a God like that either. In fact I don't know anybody who does."[3]

BELIEF IN GOD AS CRUELTY TO THE SELF

It was the German philosopher Friedrich Nietzsche who argued that humanity has always had a compelling need to justify its own existence and because of this has generated belief in a higher purpose in life. Because people are not satisfied with the notion that there is no meaning in anything, they barricade themselves away from nihilism's question "Why live at all?" with the idea of God. God, the changeless omnipotent being independent of this world, gives us transcendent universal values about good and evil and instills value in every human life with the *imago Dei*.

Nietzsche argued that because Christianity is focused on the rewards or punishments that await in the next life, the experience of life is damaged. His vision was to replace this worldview with a joyful affirmation of life. Nietzsche expounded the doctrine of *eternal recurrence*, which places one's own life and happiness as the sole consideration when evaluating how one should act.

This is placed in stark contrast with the Christian view of an afterlife, which would emphasize later reward at the cost of immediate happiness. Nietzsche characterized altruistic, "selfless" behavior as immense cruelty to oneself by imposing another's will over oneself, and he offered this as an argument against Christianity and monotheism in general. This idea of Christianity as dangerous because it is cruel to the self, denying and limiting the individual's passions, led to Nietzsche drawing up a naturalistic alternative to traditional religion.

THE DEATH OF GOD

Nietzsche announced in his work *The Gay Science* what he called "the death of God." What he meant by this is that God had died in the hearts of modern men. The idea of God was being killed off by rationalism and science.

Have you not heard of that madman who lit a lantern in the bright morning hours, ran to the market-place, and cried incessantly: "I am looking for God! I am looking for God!" As many of those who did not believe in God were standing together there, he excited considerable laughter. Have you lost him, then? said one. Did he lose his way like a child? said another. Or is he hiding? Is he afraid of us? Has he gone on a voyage? or emigrated? . . .

"Where has God gone?" he cried. "I shall tell you. We have killed him—you and I. We are his murderers. But how have we done this? How were we able to drink up the sea? Who gave us the sponge to wipe away the entire horizon? What did we do when we unchained the earth from its sun? Whither is it moving now? Whither are we moving now? Away from all suns? Are we not perpetually falling? Backward, sideward, forward, in all directions? Is there any up or down left? Are we not straying as through an infinite nothing? Do we not feel the breath of empty space? Has it not become colder? Is it not more and more night coming on all the time? Must not lanterns be lit in the morning? Do we not hear anything yet of the noise of the gravediggers who are burying God? Do we not smell anything yet of God's decomposition? Gods too decompose. God is dead. God remains dead. And we have killed him. How shall we, murderers of all murderers, console ourselves? That which was the holiest and mightiest of all that the world has yet possessed has bled to death under our knives. Who will wipe this blood off us? With what water could we purify ourselves? What festivals of atonement, what sacred games shall we need to invent? Is not the greatness of this deed too great for us? Must we not ourselves become gods simply to be worthy of it? There has never been a greater deed; and whosoever shall be born after us—for the sake of this deed he shall be part of a higher history than all history hitherto."[4]

Nietzsche understood that the "death of God" idea would also involve the ending of universal standards of morality as well as the end of any sense of meaning or purpose in life. And so the "dangerous" or "cruel" God-hypothesis was to be replaced by a naturalistic worldview. This supposedly superior worldview was to liberate humanity from the constraints of Christianity by creating a new set of values most clearly seen in his idea of the *ubermensch,* or "superman."

I teach you the *ubermensch.* Man is something that shall be overcome. What have you done to overcome him? All beings so far have created something beyond themselves; and do you want to be the ebb of this great flood and even go back to the beasts rather than overcome man? What is the ape to man? A laughingstock or a painful embarrassment. And man shall be just that for the overman: a laughingstock or a painful embarrassment.[5]

The "superman" trusts what he finds within himself; he creates his own good and evil, based on whatever helps him to succeed rather than fail. Good is that which enables one to fulfill one's potential, and evil is whatever stands in the way of this. To Nietzsche, everything in the world is transitory and the superman embraces this idea of change. To keep up with the times, he is constantly reinventing himself over and over, always building something stronger, more powerful, on top of what went before. The source of his strength lies in the natural desires of humans, which Nietzsche sees as restricted in Christianity. Sex is "a great invigoration of the heart"; the lust to rule is a "gift giving virtue" because it allows new ideas to come to the fore; selfishness is "blessed, wholesome [and] healthy."[6] He sees these desires as the best of all possible good, since they act as the driving force behind man's insatiable need to overcome, enabling him to rise above the masses (the weaker, the unwise). Once at the top, the superman can serve as the example for the rest of society.

This alternative to Christianity, which relativizes good and evil—placing morality at the whim of individual likes and dislikes and glorifying the strident, powerful self—reveals the emptiness of the charge that Christianity is "dangerous." While looking ahead into the twentieth century, Nietzsche predicted that following his "death of God" idea there would be rivers of blood. It is ironic that atheists still call belief in God dangerous when this alternative at least is so potentially violent.

FUNDAMENTALISM

If atheism provides us with such "dangerous" philosophy as Nietzsche's, can't it still be said that religious fundamentalism is a great danger in our world. With the rise of militant Islam at the beginning of the twenty-first century, this question has become more nuanced for the Christian, since many people now equate violent Islamist groups with evangelical Christianity. The logic surely follows that since the Islamist groups base their beliefs and actions on an uncritical acceptance of their holy book,[7] it must be equally dangerous for Christians to take their holy book seriously. But this is simply not the case.

The contrasts between the New Testament—in particular, Jesus' teaching—and the teachings and actions of Muhammad are startling. Jesus refused to be a part of any political violence and did not even resist his own arrest and violent death. Muhammad led others out in bloody battles, instigated the killing of opponents, and he wrote in the Qur'an the verses that still inspire Islamist groups today.

Last year, while speaking at the White House, I was asked by a West Wing staff member, "Our president said that Islam is a peaceful religion. What do you think?" Here was a difficult moment. Having studied Islam, and militant Islam in particular, I found it quite awkward to answer briefly. I said, "Politicians have to make statements which they know will have huge ramifications. Your president will have had community relations in mind when he said this. It is true that many Muslims are peaceful and that some verses in the Qur'an encourage this in certain contexts. However, it is not possible to deny that other devout Muslims use violence as an outworking of their faith, and this is following their holy book and their prophet. We cannot ignore these facts. On this basis I would not choose 'peaceful' as a useful generic catch-all phrase to describe Islam as a religion."

A brief discussion of definitions of the term *fundamentalism* may be important here because use of the word ranges from the technical to the pejorative. Historically *fundamentalism* finds its roots within Protestantism in America and Britain in the late nineteenth century, especially among Brethren and Baptist denominations, and it must be seen to be working alongside other theological streams such as Dispensationalism, Pentecostalism and the Holiness movement, which arose from the same era and came to prominence in the 1920s.[8] After this time, *fundamentalism* became a descriptive label, and since the 1970s, it increasingly has been used to denote movements and theologies in other religious communities, particularly in Islam.

Even in the contemporary era, there is a noticeable disparity from one side of the Atlantic to the other. In some church circles in America, *fundamentalism* still retains the initially positive meaning of holding to the fundamentally important principles and aspects of the faith; in Europe, it is uncertain whether *fundamentalism* could really be used in a nonpejorative sense outside the confines of academic theology.

Where sensitive scholarship has attempted to clarify *fundamentalism*, it has been defined simply as "the belief in old traditional forms of religion, or the belief that what is written in a holy book is completely true."[9] The majority of the adherents of all the major world religions would be "fundamentalist" if this catch-all understanding were maintained. This definition is also in danger of historical anachronism, for there would be little to differentiate a traditional, pre-Enlightenment approach to the Scriptures from a fundamentalist one.

Another explanation of what is meant by *fundamentalism*, which places it more firmly in the modern era, calls fundamentalism "a usually religious movement or point of view characterized by a return to fundamental principles, by rigid adherence to those principles and often by intolerance of other views and opposition to secularism."[10]

Here fundamentalism is described with reference to both its creative and its resistant elements. Creatively it involves a *return* to fundamental principles—in a context where the believing community seems to have disregarded them—and then a tenacious allegiance to those principles once they have been established. This, it is then argued, cannot be expressed without resisting what is perceived to be its opposites in other ideologies and expressly in secularism. Thus it follows that the key to fundamentalism is not the intolerant stance taken, but the principles decided on in the first place.

Defining *fundamentalism*, even within Islam alone, let alone more widely, is notoriously difficult.

> "Fundamentalists" also want to interpret Islam in terms of original sources of authority in the light of contemporary needs, but they strongly object to any attempt or tendency to "Westernise" Islam. For them the shariah is indeed flexible and capable of development to meet changing need, but interpretation and development must be done in a genuinely Islamic manner, and must not involve covert forms of Westernising. They also criticise many of the traditional ways and practices, but even more they object to the tendency of many traditionalists to tolerate and even co-operate with secularising governments in practise.[11]

It seems that *fundamentalism* is a catch-all term, which, though popular in the media, has been resisted in more recent years by scholars.[12] The desire for a resurgent Islamic society and political system is fairly universal, but the militant, or as they are better termed "Islamist," groups have certain convictions about how the Islamic rebirth might best be achieved.[13] Daniel Pipes defines Islamism as

> an ideology that demands man's complete adherence to the sacred law of Islam and rejects as much as possible outside influence, with some exceptions (such as access to military and medical technology). It is imbued with a deep antagonism towards non-Muslims and has a particular hostility towards the West. It amounts to an effort to turn Islam, a religion and civilization, into an ideology.[14]

Two things might be said here. First, to the extent to which fundamentalism involves intolerance of others, Christians reject it. Second, the act of merely returning to fundamental principles is in and of itself neutral. It may be positive or negative; one simply cannot adjudicate without first examining the principles themselves. However, it is especially important for Christians to respond sensitively to charges of fundamentalism in a culture where the two forces of militant Islam and rampant secularism are clashing. A helpful Christian solution *tolerare malus* (tolerate evil) was developed by Augustine and Aquinas. Within this model, Christians present Christ powerfully and boldly as different from any other alternative and also go on upholding the right of others to think, reason, teach, inform and disagree.

Tolerare Malus

The practice of toleration is an openness toward what is true, recognizing that the truth of God is true for all people, but without fear of disagreement. An example of this early practice is found in Justin Martyr (ca. 100-ca. 165), who came to the Christian faith by way of Stoicism and Platonism. For him, Christian faith is the "touchstone" of truth. He believed that the identification of Christ as *Logos* in Scripture opened the way to understanding even pre-Christian philosophies as bearing a measure of truth. Historian Henry Chadwick explains, "Christ is for Justin the principle of unity and the criterion by which we may judge the truth, scattered like divided seeds among the different schools of philosophy in so far as they have dealt with religion and morals."[15]

Clement of Alexandria (ca. 150-ca. 215) provides another witness. Like Philo on behalf of Judaism more than a century before, he incorporated the best works of Hellenistic literature and philosophy in his Christian teaching. The writings of Clement that have survived contain more than seven hundred quotations from more than three hundred pagan sources. At the same time, it was perfectly clear that Scripture was his authority. His arguments would explore the world of Homer or Heraclitus, but then he would resolve the issue beginning with the words "it is written." His thought was not syncretistic, but synthetic. There was, for him, a "chorus of truth" on which the Christian might draw. Alternative sources did not replace Scripture, but illuminated its pages and could be read alongside it.

Voltaire wrote in 1763, "Of all religions, the Christian is undoubtedly that which should instill the greatest toleration, although so far the Christians have been the most intolerant of all men."[16]

Augustine used the concept of *tolerare malus* to mean putting up with evil for the sake of the greater good. In his writings against the Manichaeans and the Donatists, who were groups he found himself in opposition to, he asks them whether it might not "for the sake of the peace of Donatus, (be better) to put up with the most flagrant and notorious wickedness of Optatus."[17] He goes on to draw a distinction between those who do sinful things and those who do not stop them:

> There is a great difference between those who consent because they take pleasure in such things, and those who tolerate while they dislike them. The former make themselves chaff, while they follow the barrenness of the chaff; the latter are the grain. Let them wait for Christ, who bears the winnowing-fan, that they may be separated from the chaff.[18]

This Christian principle underpins an important part of our Western democratic system. That is not to say that Christians do not speak out against that which is wrong, whether idea or activity, but it does mean that enemies and opponents are not obliterated by force. Notice the stark contrast with Islamic thought, in which shariah law makes little provision for those who may disagree, as can be seen by the implementation of blasphemy laws in countries such as Pakistan. Historically there has been a modified toleration within Islam where Abrahamic faith communities were allowed to live in Islamic territories if they paid a punitive tax and where they were exempted from some religious laws, but this has never allowed for conversion. Within Islam, apostasy even to an Abrahamic faith is punishable by death.

Toleration has only been practiced rarely and for relatively short periods, such as within parts of the Ottoman Empire. It is hard to point today to an Islamic country where genuine freedom and toleration exist. Saudi Arabia is viewed by a Western liberal media outlet such as the BBC as a "moderate regime." And yet a British Airways hostess was recently moved from working on long-haul routes because she wanted to carry a Bible in her possessions onto the tarmac of a Saudi airport, but was forbidden to do so.

Thomas Aquinas wrote,

> Human government is derived from the Divine government, and should imitate it. Now although God is all-powerful and supremely good, nevertheless He allows certain evils to take place in the universe, which He might prevent, lest, without them, greater goods might be forfeited, or greater evils ensue. Accordingly in human government also, those who are in authority, rightly tolerate certain evils, lest certain goods be lost, or certain greater evils be incurred.[19]

In a culture of rising secular ideologies and militant Islam, it must be possible for the Christian to distinguish the biblical worldview from these opponents and demonstrate that, far from being "dangerous," Christianity provides the very undergirding of a democratic ideal that allows debate and disagreement to function and even flourish. It was Lesslie Newbigin who wrote,

> The truth is that it is the dogma rightly understood, namely the free gift of God's grace in Jesus Christ, which alone can establish and sustain freedom of thought and

of conscience. We must affirm the gospel as truth, universal truth, truth for all peoples and for all times, the truth which creates the possibility of freedom; but we negate the gospel if we deny the freedom in which alone it can be truly believed.[20]

9

I Used to Believe, but I've Given It All Up

I recently went to give a lecture about the Christian mind to a group of Christian women on the south coast of England. They were a delightful group—these formidable women are made of the same stuff as their ancestors, who helped their country win two world wars and were the backbone of the British Empire. Having referred in my lecture to a statistical survey of declining church attendance in Great Britain, I asked how many people in the room had children and/or grandchildren who were no longer practicing Christians. Eighty percent raised their hands.

At the end of the meeting, I heard story after story of individuals who had drifted away from the church or of those who had vehemently turned their backs on their families' beliefs. Since my usual experience involves direct contact with skeptics and those who have questions about the Christian faith, it was rather poignant to see it all from this different perspective—mothers and grandmothers who were weeping over their relatives, but were at a complete loss as to how to deal with the questions or concerns of these loved ones.

There are, of course, many reasons people turn away from Christianity, but in this chapter I want us to examine some of the most common ones.

I'VE GROWN OUT OF IT; I'M MORE SOPHISTICATED NOW

Tony Benn, who was raised by a fervent Christian mother, has gone on to be a much-loved socialist politician in the U.K. House of Commons, a champion of the marginalized and less fortunate in society. He reflected on his childhood experiences of hearing the Bible being read out by his mother and commented in a BBC radio broadcast, "My mother taught us that in the Old Testament there were kings and prophets. The kings were interested in power and the prophets cried out for justice. She told us, 'Make sure you are always on the side of the prophets.' "[1] Although not a Christian believer himself, he remembered his mother's influence fondly, but now espouses a more "liberal" outlook.

It is not unusual to meet people who have moved on from their childhood roots in Christianity and who view it with a mixture of nostalgia for days gone by and superiority, feeling that they have left such naive and unsophisticated ways behind them. It may be useful for such people to encounter the challenge of Christ afresh as adults and to consider whether they have subjected their own post-Christian worldview to serious scrutiny. As Alister McGrath puts it,

> Although I was passionately and totally persuaded of
> the relevance of atheism as a young man, I subsequently
> found myself persuaded that Christianity was a much
> more interesting and intellectually exciting worldview
> than atheism. I have always valued free thinking and be-
> ing able to rebel against the orthodoxies of an age. Yet I
> never suspected where my free thinking would take me.[2]

The crucial question to be faced here is whether the Christian worldview merits serious investigation; whether I went
to church as a child or not, does Christianity make sense and,
more importantly, is it actually true?

I DON'T BELIEVE IT IS TRUE ANYMORE

Debating someone on the radio is a daunting affair. Not only
are you trying to position yourself correctly for the micro-
phone, keep your eye on the time and listen to the instruc-
tions of your host, you are also engaging in a debate with an
individual in the same studio with the added dynamic of an
invisible listening audience.

It was in such a setting that I encountered a man who had
abandoned his Christian faith after many years and embraced
an atheistic worldview. His journey to unbelief had been
prompted by reading a book by a Christian whom he felt was
dishonest with a particular fact. Once this happened, he began
to distrust everything else he had read or been told. And once
he had rejected Christianity, he wholeheartedly embraced
atheism. As we discussed various issues, this man seemed
unaware that he had swapped one set of presuppositions for

another, and he was reluctant to subject his new atheistic position to any scrutiny at all.

I STILL WONDER WHETHER CHRISTIANITY IS TRUE OR NOT

It was Einstein who said, "What you call a fact depends on the theory you bring to it." This is crucial in any discussion, be it scientific, legal or philosophical. Unless we are prepared to examine the assumptions we are making and the interpretive framework being used, we are on dangerous ground. Many people who are skeptical about Christianity are inconsistent when it comes to appraising their own viewpoint. It is as if Christians are completely biased, trying to impose their views on others but non-Christian thinkers occupy a neutral space of free thinking.

There is no such neutral space. Such non-Christian thinkers have their own assumptions in equal measure. The presuppositions of secularism—that there is no God, miracles do not happen and man is the measure of all things—need to be challenged and questioned as rigorously as the Christian presuppositions—that the God who created the world and made humanity in his image is a personal being who reveals himself. Which presuppositions most adequately account for the universe, reason, personhood and all that we see and experience?

The first question to establish then is whether the Christian worldview corresponds with reality. Does the Bible accurately describe the real world—morally, philosophically and historically? Does it diagnose the human condition convincingly? Does it provide us with insight into the origin and purpose of the universe? We need to read the Bible—perhaps beginning with the Gospels as a good starting place—to meaningfully answer these questions. The Christian philosopher and apologist Francis Schaeffer writes:

> With the propositional communication from the personal God before us not only the things of the cosmos and history match up but everything on the upper and lower stories matches too: grace and nature; a moral absolute and morals; the universal point of reference and the particulars; and the emotional and aesthetic realities of man as well.[3]

These crucial questions about the relevance and consistency of the Christian worldview will help to establish whether Christianity provides an adequate basis for thought and life. Of course these questions must be asked of all the competing alternatives, not just the Christian worldview.

Once we have examined competing presuppositions, I believe there is a subsequent role for examining evidence in discerning truth. I do not use the word *proof* here, because it carries connotations of repeatable scientific experiments, which cannot be produced to support naturalistic assumptions or Christian statements. But for the Christian, compelling evidence exists that points us to the validity and truthfulness of the Christian message. Evidence that can be examined today by skeptics and questioners would include the manuscript tradition of the New Testament and in particular the historical evidence around the life, death and resurrection of Christ. Examining the historical claim at the heart of the Christian faith that the man called Jesus, having been crucified on a Roman cross, was actually raised from the dead is essential in answering the question "How can I know if this is true?" If this resurrection of Jesus could be disproved, Christianity would collapse as a worldview. If, however, it emerges as the solution to which the historical evidence clearly points, it is compelling evidence, which can be dissected and examined by anyone interested, that Jesus was who he claimed to be.

The resurrection of Jesus. New Testament scholar R. T. France writes,

> It may be argued that at the level of their literary and historical character, we have good reason to treat the Gospels seriously as a source of information on the life and teaching of Jesus, and thus on the historical origins of Christianity. Ancient historians have sometimes commented that the degree of skepticism with which New Testament scholars approach their sources is far greater than would be thought justified in any other branch of ancient history. Indeed, many ancient historians would count themselves fortunate to have four such responsible accounts, written within a generation or two of the events, and preserved in such a wealth of early manuscript evidence as to be, from the point of view of textual criticism, virtually uncontested in all but detail. Beyond that point, the decision on how far a scholar is willing to accept the record they offer is likely to be influenced more by his openness to a "supernaturalist" worldview than by strictly historical considerations.[4]

What are the issues to be considered when thinking about the resurrection of Jesus?

- Jesus really did die on the cross. The Romans knew how to kill by crucifixion, and they made sure with the spear.

- Jesus was buried in a tomb belonging to a man called Joseph of Arimathea.

- The disciples were disheartened and discouraged.

- Women were not acceptable as reliable witnesses in a court of law, yet they are cited as the first witnesses, with much resting on their evidence.

- No other burial tradition exists, whether by friends of Jesus or rivals; the tomb was universally acknowledged as empty.

- The preaching of the early church, which is recorded in the book of Acts, is founded on and explained by the resurrection.

- The disciples' attitudes were transformed. They moved from fear for their own lives to great courage in proclaiming Jesus' resurrection in the face of persecution and opposition.

- The resurrected Christ appeared to large numbers of people (five hundred) after his death, including skeptical questioners (Thomas), unbelievers (James) and outright enemies (Saul/Paul).

- The disciples had no precedent for an individual resurrection in their day because Jewish theology assumed and expected a corporate resurrection in the end times. It is unlikely that they would have made this up.

None of these points alone prove the resurrection, but cumulatively they are most reasonably explained by it. But what are the alternative possibilities when it comes to Jesus' resurrection?

The first possibility is that Jesus did actually die, but the

apostles were deceived about his resurrection. They hallu-
cinated the resurrection appearances after some unknown
party stole the body of Jesus. There are major problems with
this theory: Who stole the body? Was that even possible, given
the huge stone and the guard? Why didn't they ever produce
the body to put an end to the Christian religion? How could
five hundred simultaneously have had the same hallucina-
tion? These are important questions. If we are to reject Christianity, can we overcome these difficulties with the alternative
explanations that are sometimes offered for the empty tomb
of Christ?

A further alternative possibility offered by some to the resurrection of Christ is that after Jesus died, the disciples themselves stole the body. They were mythmakers conspiring to deceive the world and make others believe that Jesus had risen.
But what changed their minds from fear and self-preservation
to be prepared to go out and die for a lie? How did they get the
body out of a sealed, guarded tomb? Why was there no breaking of ranks so that this lie would eventually come out?

A third possibility is that Jesus didn't die; in fact, he came
to in the cool of the tomb, wriggled out of his grave clothes,
pushed the huge stone away and overcame the guard. Known
as "the swoon," this is the least plausible due to the proficiency
of Roman soldiers at killing, the difficulty of extricating oneself
from grave clothes after serious injury and the unlikelihood of
a being strong enough to move a huge stone and overpower
Roman soldiers single-handedly following an attempted
crucifixion.

The most plausible explanation of the facts is that God raised
Jesus from the dead, not that he rose by some unknown natu-

ral process but that, because he was God's Son, death could not hold him and he was raised. If this is true, it challenges everything. As Newbigin comments,

> At the heart of the Christian message was a new fact: God had acted—and let us remember that the original meaning of *fact* is the Latin *factum,* "something done." God had acted in a way that, if believed, must henceforth determine all our ways of thinking. . . . It could not merely fit into existing ways of understanding the world without fundamentally changing them. According to Athanasius, it provided a new *arche,* a new starting point for all human understanding of the world. It could not form part of any worldview except one of which it was the basis, but at the same time, it could only be communicated to the world of classical thought by using the language of classical thought.[5]

The implications of the resurrection of Jesus are massive: this historical event will form part of a major paradigm shift in our thinking and help us build the foundations of a worldview that will shape our reasoning in every area.

Encounter. The "How can I know?" question can also be answered by a personal encounter with God. In an earlier chapter, we examined the idea of a religious delusion, but here the important point is that if God is real and Christianity is true, we can know and experience this for ourselves. Jesus says, "Here I am! I stand at the door and knock. If anyone hears my voice and opens the door, I will come in and eat with him, and he with me" (Revelation 3:20). The promise of the Bible is here and can be tested; if we ask Jesus to enter our lives and hearts, he will make himself known to us.

I DRIFTED AWAY

For some people, there are really no rational reasons to disbelieve, and there wasn't a specific moment when a decision was made to stop being a Christian; they just drifted away. They still believe in God, but life has become busier and fuller, and there really hasn't been much time for religious observance. Jesus talks about this situation in his famous parable of the sower, in which he tells of a farmer sowing seeds in different kinds of soil. One of the seeds grows well but is soon overtaken by thorns and thistles around it. These choke the seed. Jesus interprets his own parable, telling us that the thorns and thistles represent "the worries of this life and the deceitfulness of wealth" (Matthew 13:22). The urgency of Jesus' message, the reality of the judgment to come and his offer of forgiveness through the cross are in sharp relief to this kind of vague drifting. If one is going to reject Christ, at least let it be on worthwhile grounds, not just inertia.

I STRUGGLE WITH CHRISTIAN IDEAS ABOUT SEX

In our highly sexualized culture, where intimacy and sexuality are seen as inseparable, chastity is necessarily equated with loneliness. In the light of this, the radical challenge of Jesus to those who would follow him in the form of his teaching on sex is just too great. Jesus founds his teaching on sexuality in Genesis, where the divine image is expressed in both male and female. The man and woman are equally human, despite their physical, anatomical and procreative differences. As they are joined together as husband and wife, something beautiful happens: "A man will leave his father and mother and be united to his wife, and they will become one flesh" (Genesis 2:24).

Here we are given a template for human sexual love: through sexual intercourse the man and woman have a new dimension to their intimacy. This is called being "one flesh," and it is intended to be exclusive and faithful. Both Jesus and Paul pick up on this in the New Testament, emphasizing the beauty of monogamous marriage.

Although the reason for pursuing extramarital sex is a belief that it is an escape from loneliness and an embracing of intimacy, the Bible teaches that the opposite happens. Outside the protection of the commitment of marriage, multiple relationships lead to pain, brokenness and a decreasing ability to truly open up and bare one's soul to another person, for fear of being hurt.

However, I have encountered different individuals who were sexually active with their boyfriend or girlfriend, prioritizing that over Jesus' teaching, and they have ended up feeling they have committed an unforgivable sin. This may be due in part to a tendency within churches to emphasize the dangers of sexual sin and present it as worse than any other wrongdoing. Yet we see from the Bible that those who fall in this area can be restored and forgiven. This does not mean that the consequences of those actions are wiped out, whether that be pain, personal brokenness, destroyed marriages or abandonment of children. But it does mean that a relationship with God can be restored and forgiveness received.

I met a woman recently who had grown up in a Christian family; she loved God and followed Jesus. After leaving school, she fell in with a new group of friends and met a much older man whom she thought was wonderfully charming. She ended up having sex with him, and after he had ended their relationship, she discovered she was pregnant. He wasn't interested in becoming a father, and she had never imagined life as a single parent, but she decided to keep the baby. During all this time, she hardly thought about God; she was focused on her own survival and her new way of life.

It was when her daughter was three that she began to feel drawn back to church. Initially she worried about what people would think of her, but she soon rediscovered the reality of God's love. Now she and her daughter are following Jesus together. Return and restoration are possible; the heart of the Christian message is Jesus' offer of forgiveness to us.

THE MOST IMPORTANT REASON TO RETURN

Whether intellectual, moral or experiential, there are various reasons for turning away from the Christian faith, but I would like to give the most important reason to consider returning: Christianity is true and real. Everything else flows from this: if Jesus is who he claimed to be, if he rose from the dead and really does save us from our sins, if he is personally knowable today, then it would be madness to reject him. If these things are not true and real, it is right to ignore his claims as irrelevant.

The crucial question to settle then is, on what grounds have I rejected Christianity? Are these grounds substantial or circumstantial? Shouldn't I examine my presuppositions as well as the evidence for Christ before rejecting something so important out of hand?

10

How Can I Know?

IS IT ALL IN THE MIND?

A number of my friends have said to me over the years, "I'm happy for you that your Christian faith means so much to you. That's great for you, but it isn't my thing." In the twenty-first century, if we tell someone that we have a religious faith, this is usually accepted as a "good thing" but is not necessarily seen as having any particular implications for anyone else. This is because religious faith is seen as being all in the mind. Your mind is happy with this or that idea, which is good for you, but since it isn't actually real in any objective sense, it has no relevance beyond you as an individual.

But if it really is the case that what someone believes in exists only in their mind, it isn't actually real; it is an illusion. Here we see the influence of Eastern thought at work. My colleague L. T. Jeyachandran tells the story of an Indian guru who was teaching his students out in the forest. He was teaching them that all is *maya*—illusion. Suddenly a wild elephant came charging toward them, and all the students ran to escape. The guru climbed a tree and hid in the branches until the danger had passed.

When questioned about this by one of his students—"If everything is an illusion, why did you hide from the elephant?"—he answered, "Everything is an illusion. The elephant is an illusion and my running away from the elephant is an illusion. Everything is an illusion." This reveals that this philosophy is unlivable, for we all live and make decisions at least as if some things are real. Ravi Zacharias is often heard saying, "Even in India we look both ways before crossing the street. It's either the bus or me."

But if this philosophy of illusion is unlivable, isn't it also incoherent? Michael Ramsden has commented that if everything is an illusion, you must assume that there is such a thing as reality in order to distinguish illusion from reality. If there is such a thing as reality then it necessarily follows that everything can't be illusion. You affirm the existence of that which you are trying to deny.

BUT CAN WE REALLY KNOW ANYTHING?

I once heard a student say, "You cannot be certain about anything!" to which another student replied, "Are you certain about that?" It was Descartes who famously said, "I think, therefore I am"—I can know that I at least exist to do the thinking. Another common way of phrasing this question about whether it is really possible to know anything is to ask, "When a tree falls in the middle of a forest and there is no one there to hear it, does it make any noise?" This is crucial because it gets to the heart of the matter: whether there is a mind-independent reality or not. Does anything exist that is independent of and external to our minds? Or does everything exist solely within our brain?

IMMANUEL KANT

Before the philosophy of Immanuel Kant gained influence, it was generally accepted that a real world of real objects existed and the human mind responded to and analyzed that which was actually there. Kant challenged this view that a real world exists independent of the human mind and argued that instead of our thinking conforming to the world of objects, the world conforms to our way of thinking. Kant said that the categories of the mind are fixed and determine everything else. Therefore, although we can be certain of what is in our mind, we cannot be certain of what is beyond that. When we look at something, our perception only gives us the appearance of that thing. We do not know how something really is; all we can know is how it appears to us.

But an important question to be asked here is, is it possible to remove the object and still get that same perception? Doesn't this strongly imply that instead of the existence of the object being dependent on my seeing it, my seeing it is dependent on it actually existing? The reality of the world and our capacity as humans to respond to the objects and people around us underlies a Christian epistemology.[1]

The Christian worldview presents a real, personal God who creates a real world within which diverse creatures, beings and objects actually exist and interact. This God then reveals himself within his world. We as humans are then able to respond to that revelation or not. Within this paradigm, the human mind is capable of real thought and choice, but that thinking is not the sole conduit of reality.[2]

RELATIONAL KNOWLEDGE

But there is more to knowing than rational thought. For humans, there is a personal dimension to knowledge, particularly in the whole area of relationships. At its heart, Christianity claims to be about relationship. The being of God himself is trinitarian and therefore relational at his heart. He is three in one—Father, Son and Holy Spirit—existing eternally in relationship. The offer of forgiveness to humanity through Christ's death is the offer of restored relationship between us and God. This kind of personal knowledge is difficult to pin down. But it is at the heart of a true Christian faith. Ken Costa writes of his friend the visionary clergyman Sandy Millar that he had at certain times "osteo-epistemology," or "I know it in my bones."

This is where we really come down to the radical claim of Jesus: that you and I can know God. We can call him Father, and we can know his presence through the Holy Spirit whom Jesus promised would come to us. We can experience him in the depths of our hearts, as the apostle Paul wrote, "I pray that out of his glorious riches he may strengthen you with power through his Spirit in your inner being." And we can encounter his love and "grasp how wide and long and high and deep is the love of Christ, and to know this love that surpasses knowledge" (Ephesians 3:16, 18-19). This is the claim of the Christian faith: you can know God and you can know in your deepest heart of hearts that you know him.

My husband, Frog, recalls his schoolboy experiences of religion, which involved formal liturgical services and lifeless preaching. He remembers watching a clergyman at the front of church and thinking, *What an awful job that must be!* But he also wondered about the claims of Christianity: if these things were really true, oughtn't that be the most important thing in the world; shouldn't it inspire passion, joy, energy and service? Believing that Jesus is who he claimed to be and that he has risen from the dead, it was while Frog was wondering about the impact this should make that he encountered Christ for himself.

He wrote that night in his journal, "I saw a vision of Jesus on his throne and I just knew that he loved me. This love filled me. Meeting God was like electricity flooding through my body. . . . I wonder whether I should be a vicar?" This personal experience of God changed everything; now there was a reason to live, to worship, to study and to serve.

BLAISE PASCAL

The great mathematician and thinker Blaise Pascal also had an encounter with God that impacted him deeply. On Monday, November 23, 1654, he wrote,

> From about half past ten in the evening until about half
>   past midnight.
> Fire.
> God of Abraham, God of Isaac, God of Jacob, not of
>   philosophers and scholars.
> Certainty, certainty, heartfelt, joy, peace.

God of Jesus Christ.
God of Jesus Christ. . . .
Let me not be cut off from him forever.
He can only be kept by the ways taught in the Gospel.
Sweet and total renunciation.
Total submission to Jesus Christ and my director.
Everlasting joy in return for one day's effort on earth.
I will not forget thy word. Amen.[3]

Pascal pinned this written statement into the inside of his jacket over his heart and wore it there every day until he died.

Not every Christian has such a dramatic experience of God as Pascal, although many do, but the offer to all is the possibility of knowing God in a relationship in addition to knowing something about him. This is the ultimate way of finding out the answer to the question "But is it real?"—encountering God for yourself.

Notes

Chapter 1: What About Other People's Genuine Experience of God?

[1]Charles Colson, *Born Again* (Old Tappan, N.J.: Chosen Books, 1976), pp. 124, 129-30.

[2]Mahardika, "International Conference on Prophet Mohammed and His Message" (London, April 12-15, 1980), quoted in Frog and Amy Orr-Ewing, *Holy Warriors: A Fresh Look at the Face of Extreme Islam* (Carlisle, U.K.: Paternoster, 2002), p. 4.

[3]Islamic Sufism is an important exception to this rule, although Sufis are a tiny part of the Islamic faith and can be fiercely persecuted as "un-islamic" by other Muslims from the more mainstream Sunni traditions and Wahabi Islam.

[4]Annemarie Schimmel and Abdoldjavad Falaturi, *We Believe in One God* (New York: Seabury Press, 1979), p. 85.

[5]Steve Turner, "Creed," *Up to Date* (London: Hodder & Stoughton), quoted in Ravi Zacharias, *Can Man Live Without God?* (Dallas: Word Publishing, 1994), p. 42.

[6]Oxford Dictionaries, s.v. "tolerate" <www.askoxford.com/concise_oed/tolerate?view=uk>.

[7]Roger Scruton, *Modern Philosophy: An Introduction and Survey* (New York: Penguin, 1996), p. 6.

Chapter 2: Your "Experience of God" Is Delusional, Not Real . . .

[1]Richard Dawkins, *The God Delusion* (London: TransWorld Publishers, 2006), p. 88.

[2]Gordy Slack, "The Atheist," Salon.com, <http://dir.salon.com/story/news/feature/2005/04/30/dawkins/index.html?pn=2> (accessed January 11, 2008).

[3]Sam Harris, *The End of Faith: Religion, Terror and the Future of Reason* (New York: Norton, 2004), p. 72.

[4]Richard Harries, "Science does not challenge my faith," *The Observer*, April 16, 2006 <http://observer.guardian.co.uk/comment/story/0,,1754798,00.html>.

[5]Alister McGrath, *Dawkins' God* (Oxford: Blackwell, 2005), p. 9.

[6]Andrew Brown, "Dawkins the dogmatist," *Prospect*, October 2006 <www.prospect-magazine.co.uk/article_details.php?id=7803>.

[7]John Lennox, *God's Undertaker: Has Science Buried God?* (Oxford: Lion Hudson, 2007), p. 18.

[8]McGrath, *Dawkins' God*, p. 55.

[9]Dawkins, *God Delusion*, p. 55.

[10]McGrath, *Dawkins' God*, p. 55.

[11]Francis Collins, review of *Dawkins' God* <www.atheistdelusion.net/books.php>.

[12]Lennox, *God's Undertaker*, p. 33.

[13]Dawkins, *God Delusion*, p. 278.

[14]Ibid., p. 315.

[15]Sam Harris, *Letter to a Christian Nation* (New York: Alfred A. Knopf, 2006), p. 90.

[16]From *The Root of All Evil*, a television documentary on Channel 4 in the U.K. in January 2006.

[17]Quoted in Dawkins, *God Delusion*, p. 326.

[18]Lennox, *God's Undertaker*, p. 179.

[19]McGrath, *Dawkins' God*, p. 136.

[20]This became all too clear when Lennox debated Dawkins, hosted by the Fixed Point Foundation in Birmingham, Alabama, October 3, 2007.

Chapter 3: Your Relationship with God Is Just a Psychological Crutch!

[1]Letter from Sigmund Freud to Eduard Silberstein, April 11, 1875 <www.pep-web.org/document.php?id=zbk.029.0109a> or <www.boundless.org/2001/departments/pages/a0000588.html>.

[2]Armand Nicholi, *The Question of God: C. S. Lewis and Sigmund Freud Debate God, Love, Sex, and the Meaning of Life* (New York: Free Press, 2002), pp. 21-22.

[3]Sigmund Freud, *The Future of an Illusion*, trans. Peter Gay (New York: Norton, 1961), p. 30.

[4]Ibid., p. 21.

[5]Alister McGrath and Joanna Collicutt McGrath, *The Dawkins Delusion?* (Downers Grove, Ill.: InterVarsity Press, 2007), pp. 8-10.

[6]Nicholi, *Question of God*, p. 46.

[7]Ibid., p. 82.

[8]C. S. Lewis, *Miracles* (New York: Macmillan, 1960), p. 155.

[9]Ibid., p. 47.

[10]Blaise Pascal, *Pensées* (New York: Penguin, 1995), p. 45.

[11]Augustine, *Confessions* (book 1) <http://www.newadvent.org/fathers/110101.htm>, accessed January 11, 2008.

[12]The Quotations Page <www.quotationspage.com/quote/48.html>, accessed January 11, 2008. However, atheists like Simon Blackburn would claim that beauty lies within the atheist worldview.

[13]I would suggest examining cosmological, ontological, moral, historical and personal arguments for the existence of God.

[14]Freud, *Future of an Illusion*, p. 26.

[15]Ibid., p. 42.

[16]Ibid., p. 53.

[17]Kristin Rupert, "Freud and Lewis: Signs of the Supernatural," accessed online at <http://www.new-life.net/Freud.htm> on August 6, 2008.

[18]Nicholi, *Question of God*, p. 72.

[19]Freud, *Future of an Illusion*, p. 35.

[20]C. S. Lewis, *Letters to Malcolm: Chiefly on Prayer* (New York: Harcourt, 1992), p. 73.

Chapter 4: How Can You Say You Have Found the Truth If You Haven't Tried All the Alternatives?

[1]D. Pannick, QC, *The Times*, June 2, 1998.

[2]Lesslie Newbigin, *The Gospel in a Pluralist Society* (Grand Rapids: Eerdmans, 1989), p. 17.

[3]Lesslie Newbigin, *Discovering Truth in a Changing World* (London: Alpha International, 2003), pp. 12-13, emphasis added.

[4]Joanne Harris, *Chocolat* (New York: Penguin, 2000), p. 172.

[5]John Hick, *Truth and Dialogue* (London: Sheldon Press, 1974), p. 148.

Chapter 5: If Christianity Is About Relationship with God, Why Does He Let Bad Things Happen to His Friends?

[1]My current favorites on the Christian bumper-sticker market at the moment are "Carpenter requires joiners" and "Come the rapture, can I have your car?"

[2]Richard Dawkins, *River Out of Eden: A Dominion View of Life* (New York: Basic Books/HarperCollins, 1995), pp. 132-33.

[3]Arthur Koestler, *The Lotus and the Robot* (London: Hutchinson, 1960), p. 274.

[4]Frog and Amy Orr-Ewing, *Holy Warriors: A Fresh Look at the Extreme Face of Islam* (Carlisle, U.K.: Authentic, 2002), p. 8.

[5]C. S. Lewis, *Mere Christianity* (New York: HarperCollins, 1980), p. 48.

[6]Ibid., p. 50.

[7]Comments said to a journalist, "Hoddle Sacked," *BBC News*, February 3, 1999 <news.bbc.co.uk/2/hi/sport/football/270194.stm>.

[8]*Islamist* is a technical term describing a purist form of Islam, which is trying to return to earlier original models of Islam.

[9]It is important to note that Christian martyrdom is framed in the context of the martyr as the victim of violence and not its perpetrator.

[10]C. S. Lewis, *The Problem of Pain* (New York: HarperCollins, 1996), pp. 110-11.

[11]Ibid., p. 90.

[12]And so the Lord's Prayer includes the future expectation "your kingdom come" (Luke 11:2).

Chapter 6: If Christianity Is About a Transforming Relationship with God, Why Are Christians So Bad?

[1]Simon Coupland, *Spice Up Speaking* (London: Monarch, 2000), p. 135.

[2]Merriam-Webster Online, s.v. "hypocrite" <www.merriam-webster.com/dictionary/hypocrite>.

[3]Fyodor Dostoyevsky, quoted in Martin Manser, *The Westminster Collection of*

Christian Quotations (Louisville, Ky.: Westminster John Knox, 2001), p. 205.

[4]Quoted in Henry Porry Liddon, "Liddon's Bowpton Lectures 1866," (London: Rivingtons, 1869), p. 148.

[5]Thomas Merton, ed., *Gandhi on Non-Violence* (New York: New Directions, 1965), p. 34.

[6]Blaise Pascal, *Pensées* (New York: Penguin, 1995), p. 131.

Chapter 7: If God Is So Loving and Relational, Why Did He Go Ahead and Create When He Knew People Would End Up in Hell?

[1]Richard Owen, "The Fires of Hell Are Real and Eternal, Pope Warns," *The Times* (London), March 27, 2007 <www.timesonline.co.uk/tol/news/world/europe/article1572646.ece>, describing the play by John-Paul Sartre, *Closed Doors* (1944), published in the U.S. as *No Exit and Three Other Plays* (New York: Vintage, 1989).

[2]Woody Allen, "My Philosophy," in *Getting Even* (New York: Vintage, 1978).

[3]"Pope Proclaims Hell 'Exists and Is Eternal,' " *New York Post,* March 26, 2007 <www.nypost.com/seven/03262007/news/worldnews/pope_proclaims _hell_exists_and_is_eternal_worldnews_.htm>.

[4]Richard Owen, "The Fires of Hell Are Real and Eternal, Pope Warns," *The Times* (London), 27 March 2007 <www.timesonline.co.uk/tol/news/world/europe/article1572646.ece>.

[5]C. S. Lewis, *The Problem of Pain* (New York: HarperCollins, 1996), p. 27.

[6]Thomas Aquinas, *Summa Theologiae, Volume 27 (1a2ae. 86-89): Effects of Sin, Stain and Guilt,* translated by T. C. O'Brien (New York: Cambridge University Press, 2006), p. 25 (87.4).

[7]C. S. Lewis, *Problem of Pain,* p. 124.

[8]Ibid., p. 130.

Chapter 8: Belief in God Is Dangerous

[1]*Love and Death,* written and directed by Woody Allen, 85 min., MGM Studios, 1975, videocassette and DVD.

[2]Richard Dawkins, *The God Delusion* (London: TransWorld Publishers, 2006), p. 31.

[3]Alister McGrath and Joanna Collicutt McGrath, *The Dawkins Delusion?* (Downers Grove, Ill.: InterVarsity Press, 2007), p. 75.

[4]Friedrich Nietzsche, *The Gay Science* (New York: Vintage, 1974), pp. 181-82.

[5]Friedrich Nietzsche, *Thus Spoke Zarathustra* (New York: Penguin, 1974), p. 4.

[6]Ibid., p. 71.

[7]During an interview with members of the Taliban in 1996, their answer to the question posed by my fellow journalist F. Orr-Ewing "What writings have influenced your movement?" was "Only the Qur'an; no other writings interest us."

[8]For further reading, see Harriet Harris, *Fundamentalism and Evangelicals* (New York: Oxford University Press, 1998).

[9]*Cambridge International Dictionary of English,* s.v. "Fundamentalism" <dictionary.cambridge.org/define.asp?key=31735&dict=CALD>.

[10]Dictionary.com, s.v. "Fundamentalism" <dictionary.reference.com/browse /fundamentalism>.

[11]William Shepard, " 'Fundamentalism': Christian and Islamic," *Religion,* no. 17 (1987), p. 258. Also *Comments,* p. 282.

[12]*Islamisms* is plural here in keeping with the analysis of J. F. Legrain, who argues that the singular *(Islamism)* is "too monolithic, and easily categorized" (J. F. Legrain, "Palestinian Islamisms: Patriotism as a Condition of Their Expansion," in Martin Marty, *Accounting for Fundamentalisms: The Dynamic Character of Movements Palestinian Islamisms* [Chicago: University of Chicago Press, 1994], p. 413). This article also traces the "chronological analysis" of Kepel and Roy.

[13]For further discussion of Islamism, see Frog and Amy Orr-Ewing, *Holy Warriors: A Fresh Look at the Extreme Face of Islam* (Carlisle, U.K.: Authentic, 2002).

[14]Daniel Pipes, "Distinguishing Between Islam and Islamism," *Center for Strategic and International Studies,* June 30, 1998.

[15] Henry Chadwick, *Early Christian Thought and the Classical Tradition: Studies in Justin, Clement and Origen* (New York: Oxford University Press, 1984).

[16]Quoted in Harry Elmer Barnes, *An Intellectual and Cultural History of the Western World* (New York: Random House, 1937), p. 766.

[17]Augustine, *The Writings Against the Manichaeans and Against the Donatists*, vol. 4, Nicene and Post-Nicene Fathers of the Church (Whitefish, Mont.: Kessinger Publishing, 2004), p. 567.

[18]Ibid., p. 594.

[19]Thomas Aquinas *Summa Theologica* 2-2.10.11.

[20]Lesslie Newbigin, *The Gospel in a Pluralist Society* (Grand Rapids: Eerdmans, 1989), p. 10.

Chapter 9: I Used to Believe, but I've Given It All Up

[1]BBC radio broadcast.

[2]Alister McGrath and Joanna Collicutt McGrath, *The Dawkins Delusion?* Downers Grove, Ill.: InterVarsity Press, 2007), p. 9.

[3]Francis Schaeffer, *The God Who Is There* (Downers Grove, Ill.: InterVarsity Press, 1988), p. 138.

[4]R. T. France, "The Gospels as Historical Sources for Jesus, the Founder of Christianity," *Truth* 1 (1985): 86.

[5]Lesslie Newbigin, *Proper Confidence: Faith, Doubt and Certainty in Christian Discipleship* (Grand Rapids: Eerdmans, 1995), p. 4.

Chapter 10: How Can I Know?

[1]Epistemology is a theory of knowing.

[2]See J. P. Moreland, "Scaling the Secular City: A Defense of Christianity" (Grand Rapids, Baker Academic, 1987) for a helpful discussion of knowledge and paradigm.

[3]Blaise Pascal, *Pensées* (New York: Penguin, 1995), pp. 285-86.

The Zacharias Trust
is the European office of
Ravi Zacharias International Ministries (RZIM).

Ravi Zacharias International Ministries seeks to reach and challenge those who shape the ideas of a culture with the credibility and the beauty of the gospel of Jesus Christ. With a team of individuals based in six countries, RZIM is committed to reaching this generation around the world— in the university, the arts, politics, business, and the church. Through open forums, community outreach, and various media, RZIM seeks to remove the barriers to the cross for the skeptic and prepare Christians to give a reason for the hope within us.

www.zactrust.org

www.rzim.org